LEXON
BIBLE

0.3.7

DRAFT 3

Lexon is under development. The concrete facts and examples in this book will be replaced by better iterations fast. The general principles described will hold. Visit www.Lexon.tech.

BEST BEFORE APRIL 2020

0.3.7

DRAFT 3

Please send feedback to
lexon.bible@gmail.com

ISBN 978-1656262660
https://www.amazon.com/dp/1656262665

PLEASE SEND YOUR FEEDBACK,
THOUGHTS AND CRITICISM TO
LEXON.BOOK@GMAIL.COM

I AM HAPPY TO ACKNOWLEDGE
YOUR NAME IN THE CREDITS
IF YOU DON'T OBJECT

FOR UPDATES ON LEXON, JOIN THE
LEXON MAILING LIST
LIST.LEXON.TECH

TRY THE
ONLINE TUTORIAL
LEXON.TECH/TUTORIAL

WRITE AND DEPLOY CONTRACTS:
ONLINE EDITOR
DEMO.LEXON.TECH

WWW.LEXON.TECH

About Lexon

Lexon is a computer language that anyone can read.

It was made for blockchain smart contracts and can be used to write normal contracts that work as blockchain smart contracts: with Lexon, the same text is both program and legal agreement. This is useful for any organization that wants its smart contracts, or any program it uses, on- or off-chain, to be readable for all its members. It works for legal agreements as well as for internal process flow or high-level business logic. Lawmakers can write 'Robotic Laws' in it that machines can read.

Lexon is a programming language, based on advanced paradigms, implemented using mainstream compiler technology. **Find updates about Lexon at https://www.Lexon.tech.**

About this Book

In non-technical terms, this book explains Digital Contracts: legally enforceable smart contracts that anyone can read. **You do NOT need prior knowledge about blockchains.**

The book outlines the concept, gives examples, provides links to online tools that help to write, sign, deploy and manage digital contracts on the blockchain. Lexon's grammar, vocabulary and document structure are illustrated. Its paradigm is explained, including how it differs from other programming languages, staying closer to human thought. Lexon's relationship to Computational Law and AI is discussed and applications and benefits are detailed. The appendix lists notable steps towards human-readability by other programming languages, complemented with notes on constructed human languages.

There is a shorter version of this book out at
amazon.com/dp/169774768X, ISBN 978-1697747683.

Credits

Thank you for your contributions to Lexon to:

Carla Reyes, Brian Fox, Thomas Hardjono, T. J. Saw, Xenya Serova, Constance Choi, Marcelo Alaniz, Nicolas Guzzo, Benedikt Schuppli, Nikolas Guggenberger, Harald Stieber, Tom Montgomery, Yanislav Malahov, Dominic Williams, Florian Glatz, Oliver Goodenough, David Bovill, Anja Blaj, Marina Markezic, Stan Stalnaker, Ed Hesse and Dan Barnhizer.

Thank you for making this a better book to:

Carla Reyes, Florian Idelberger, Tom Montgomery, Linus Lindgren, Anja Blaj, Dazza Greenwood, Megan Ma, and Walter Berger.

Copyright

Table of Contents

DETAILED INDEX PG. 379

Introduction

Programs that anyone can read. Legalese that just works.

A new profession will rise, maybe not from the ashes, but from the very much altered, evolved body of the legal profession: the *legal engineer.*

Lexon will not replace lawyers, much less coders. But change is around the corner. Like book stores and all of retail, the internet keeps shaking up our world in fundamental ways, often hard to imagine. Entrenched players have learned the hard way that bits and bytes can be sound and light. Now, thanks to blockchain, bytes can be money.

Money more real than your money, actually. Not just bank account 'money' that any banker will tell you is but an idle promise. Money more like central bank money that today only the banks have. That's huge in itself. Lexon hypercharges it.

Contracts funnel money. Imagine they could be made to automatically, unbreakably perform. That's a smart contract. Imagine further you could write such a contract, on your computer like you always did, in plain English. And 'magically' it took care of itself, the receipts, the billing, the handling of edge cases, just as written. And as far as the payment side is concerned, it can't be broken. As connoisseurs will tell you, this changes the fundamental power equations of contracting. It will change not just legal practice but negotiations, risk estimates, financial planning, commerce. That's around the corner.

Lexon helps navigating this change, joining the old with the new, the power of the word with the power of the electron, and by this makes blockchain technology accessible in an utterly unexpected way that will touch many walks of life.

This book is for everyone who is curious and has an open mind. You will find use for Lexon that no-one thought of.

DIGITAL
CONTRACTS

This is a self-executable blockchain[1] smart contract,
and also the text of a legally enforceable agreement:

LEX Escrow.

"Payer" is a person.
"Payee" is a person.
"Agent" is a person.
"Fee" is an amount.

The Payer pays an Amount into escrow, appoints the Payee,
appoints the Agent, and also fixes the Fee.

CLAUSE: Pay Out.
The Agent may pay from escrow the Fee to themselves,
and afterwards pay the remainder of the escrow to the Payee.

CLAUSE: Pay Back.
The Agent may pay from escrow the Fee to themselves,
and afterwards return the remainder of the escrow to the Payer.

Fig 1 – Lexon code example: Escrow

---

[1] You don't need to know anything about blockchains to enjoy this book. If
you want to read up on it, check out pg. 317.

Anyone can read this text and understand what it means. It can be shown to a judge, it can be understood by business partners and customers as well as a company's management and legal department; and it can also – as is – be run as a program, for example on a blockchain, i.e. as smart contract.

Soon, any type of program can be written this way. And any type of agreement can be automated and made impossible to be broken (pg. 6). This will uncouple business necessities from the judicative and executive powers, their astronomical costs and glacial speed. Digital Contracts cost pennies to set in motion and can securely make any sum of money change hands in minutes. This will be a game changer for a massive slice of commercial activity and enable a long tail of private trade. It will also change the standards for governance and government.

Blockchain technology was made by hackers for hackers[2] – but with Lexon, anyone can read programs now without any knowledge of programming. And thus, consumers, as well as businesspeople, judges, jury members, even lawmakers,[3] can read any smart contract about which they might be tasked to decide, investigate, legislate, to verify or enter. Through this, contracting may become part of the definition of literacy and a silver arrow in the quiver of democracy.

As lawyers confirm, the code in Fig 1 *is* a legally enforceable contract: it can be used to demonstrate to a judge what the *meeting of the minds* of the parties to the contract was. There are no style requirements for a contract. There can't be any, or else a typo or poor grasp of grammar could render contracts invalid. But smart contract code e.g. written in Solidity[4] or Sophia[5] would always lead to a battle of experts if brought to court because non-programmers cannot read them.

---

[2] Vitalik Buterin, the inventor of Ethereum says he wanted to empower devs.

[3] For a real example of proposed legislation written in Lexon see pg. 71.

[4] The program language of choice for the Ethereum blockchain, see pg. 16.

[5] The program language of the Aeternity blockchain.

Not all contracts need to be in writing. The 'contract' itself is always the *abstract* agreement of two parties, no matter how it was expressed. A signed paper merely proves it. Now, a readable, digitally signed program can prove *and perform* this will.

The Document

Digital contracts are, in fact, computer programs that anyone can read because they are coded in plain English that obeys narrow limitations as to what words and grammatical rules can be used. This is called *controlled language* (see pg. 149).

An example would be:

> **The Agent may send the money in escrow to the Payee.**

Fig 2 – Lexon digital contract example sentence

This could be a sentence in a digital contract. This sentence would give some person identified as Agent the *option* to pay out the escrow, to whatever it amounts and whenever (!) the Agent feels like it. This sentence also *is* program code that when executed checks that it is really the Agent that is trying to make the payout; and that makes sure the money goes to the Payer and nowhere else. With a blockchain, there is no way that the Agent or anyone else involved could redirect it. Note how this is more powerful than an agreement with a human notary. It is also much cheaper and faster. Also note that using the special power of blockchain, this code *itself* completes the actual transfer of funds when triggered by the Agent. There is no device behind or beyond that is triggered and does the actual work. It is this very code, running on the chain, that effects the change of the relevant account balances. Accounts are in the end numbers and this code changes these numbers.

A Lexon digital contract can be embedded in legal prose: it can be part of a much larger legal document or it can be all of it (pg. 20). It consists of four parts: *head, definitions, recitals,* and *clauses* (pg. 13). There is some meta information in the *head*. The *definitions* list the parties and other names used in the contract. The *recitals* spell out what is to happen before and at the beginning of the contract. The *clauses* describe what options the parties to the contract have, and bring more definitions.

Optionality + Unbreakability

The word 'may' in the examples (Fig 1 and Fig 2) points to an elemental distinction. Digital contracts, in so far as they are *blockchain smart contracts*, cannot *coerce* any action. They can send money and log statements. They cannot otherwise force anyone to do anything. They typically operate on *incentives* instead and utilize *staking* to broaden the applicability of this principle: you may first have to pay something in that you will lose if you don't perform your role. This is why the clauses in digital contracts do not describe obligations and do not use 'must', 'shall' etc. Instead, they use 'may' and 'pay' a lot. This is a blockchain aspect that Lexon digital contracts but reflect. It is a different focus than usual for legal agreements but it is not unheard of in the world of paper contracts either. A close hard look reveals that obligations in contracts today are in reality often seen as mere options, and are treated as such, with the cost of breach being an expected part of the corporate decision matrix. This is called Efficient Breach (more about it on pg. 114).

To the extent that it lists only options, smart contract code is 'unbreakable,' the great achievement of blockchains. If in the example above, the Agent decided to *not* act, 'the blockchain' cannot prevent that. This would not count as 'breaking' this code though, which does not read 'must pay' or 'shall pay:' the example in Fig 2 just gave an option obviously, reading 'may pay.' And this option is not broken if the Agent does not pay. In a more involved example, a complementary clause could be added to handle the fine that might hit an AWOL[6] Agent. But no breach would result *no matter* how the Agent chose to act or not act. The contract could be extended so that if they don't act, they might lose a stake they had to pay in to assume the role of Agent in the first place. However, if the Agent acts, they can **only do exactly what is written**: pay the escrow to the Payee. They cannot partially pay or pay to someone else (unless there is another clause giving that option). It is within these confines that a smart contract is 'unbreakable.' This is still a game changer, especially when being honest about how contract obligations in business today are thought of as options.

These special powers, and limitations of blockchains is what leads to a focus on options instead of coercion in the prose of digital contracts. Lexon did not invent this essential feature of blockchain smart contracts, it just makes it much easier to see and to

Digital + Online

The text of a digital contract is on the one hand the legally enforceable agreement. Its function is as per usually to find clarity, to remind, and, if necessary, to serve as evidence in court. The same text is also translated by a program called the *Lexon compiler* (pg. 179) into code that can be executed on a blockchain. The digital contract is translated into a smart contract. It can be translated to different blockchains, at no cost. On the technical level, Lexon *creates* code in the language Solidity (pg. 17) to run a smart contract on the Ethereum blockchain, or in the language Sophia to run the contract on the Aeternity[7] blockchain.

---

[6] AWOL means temporarily deserted ("away without leave").

[7] Aeternity is a blockchain notable for its engineering and tight integration of oracles and state channels. – https://www.aeternity.com

The language Motoko will be added for Dfinity,[8] and other target platforms will follow. Lexon digital contracts will also be running without any blockchain involved, for the myriad of situations where trust is not an issue. The technical details are of no concern for a user of Lexon but the resulting flexibility makes an investment in Lexon code future-proof: no matter which blockchain or program language will win out, Lexon code will very likely work for it. One of the major risky decisions and up-front research tasks for any blockchain project today – what platform to use – is cancelled out. Because it is open source, it will always be possible to add what is missing or to cater to any niche that might be relevant for a specific project.

To check out more examples and experience how this works live, an online editor for Lexon digital contracts awaits at **http://demo.lexon.tech** (pg. 20). It has examples that can serve as a starting point for your own experimentation and allows to deploy your digital contracts directly to a blockchain mainnet or testnet,[9] literally at the click of a button. The contract can then be managed or test-driven using the *contract manager* that appears in your browser.

Programming Law

To some extent, Lexon solves the major challenge of Computational Law (pg. 95) by enabling a precise, digitized representation of the actual 'meaning' of a contract. By design, Lexon does not try *Deontic logic* beyond the atomic keyword 'may.' It ducks the arithmetic problems of 'shall' and 'must,' namely the ambiguity of their negations. Lexon stays with Boolean

---

[8] Dfinity promises to take the blockchain mantra of the 'Internet Computer' to the next level. – https://www.dfinity.org

[9] Blockchains have technically identical sandboxes to test smart contracts.

'true' and 'false' values instead (pg. 114), firmly based in its origin from smart contracts, which are programs.[10]

This yields surprising mileage. For very procedural parts, Lexon can even be used to articulate law (pg. 79). The home game for Lexon though are contracts including three parties, where eventually a payment is made. We will look at examples for coded law, a general service contract (pg. 83) and a complete DAO[11] (pg. 85).

The basic idea to make programs more readable by building in natural language elements has been employed since the 1950s (pg. 324). But it has not been attempted as comprehensively as Lexon proposes. The closest may be Attempto Controlled English (ACE) that was developed at the ETH Zürich in the 1990s (pg. 356), to allow for logic reasoning based on plain English input. Lexon reaches beyond this, towards programmability.

Linguistics + AI

Lexon currently has a vocabulary of about 130 words (pg. 30) and a rather small rule set based on the English subject-verb-object sentence grammar (pg. 35). This will grow and change over time. The way that a Lexon document is structured (pg. 35) is an important meta aspect of the 'grammar' of Lexon code. It has been shown to be very possible for non-programmers to learn to write Lexon. In practice, picking it up will be more similar to learning a natural language than Math or programming.[12]

---

[10] Which is a modest way to say that Lexon is based on hundreds of years of passionate research into logic that actually works. Starting at the latest with the mathematician Leibniz, son of a jurist, grandson of a professor of law.

[11] Decentralized Autonomous Organizations (DAOs) have money, rules, often human members. They are coded on a blockchain, cannot really be policed or taken down and can of course go spectacularly wrong.

[12] For a tutorial see pg. 42 and http://www.lexon.tech/tutorial

Lexon is premised on the notion that AI that can truly read, understand and process just any text is *not* around the corner. Lexon implements a different take on the relationship between language and thought than mainstream AI proposed, as linguists of late are displaying more caution in their theories about this relationship. It's not as straight forward as once hoped. Lexon uses simple linguistic models, which were in the 60s thought to be capable of explaining natural language but have instead found success in computer sciences: as the basis for tools to create program languages with. As linguistics has come full circle, Lexon employs these tools as they have since evolved in computer sciences *back* to natural language (pg. 95).

Lexon in this way 'shortcuts' the process of natural language processing and implements what could be called a *pass-through principle*: instead of trying to achieve intelligent 'understanding' of its input, it excels at leaving the fabric of its input intact all the way to the output. Instead of a 'destructive' analysis, Lexon preserves and uses the natural structure of language also internally. Logic is of course not conditional upon awareness of it, and therefore, the absence of sentience does not reduce Lexon's processing power. A lot of things can be achieved without 'understanding' their meaning. Lexon produces surprising output because it reflects the input back in a way that leaves material parts of it untouched. Accordingly, no representation of thought other than the language input itself is attempted by Lexon, i.e. no translation of meaning into bits and bytes. Instead, the basic devices of compiler building are turned on processing natural language *itself,* as if it were a program.

This breaks new ground (pg. 155) and empowers Lexon to play a pivotal role as a nexus in blockchain technology, almost as a side-effect: Lexon will be able to compute different natural languages as input – Besides English, German and Japanese have successfully been tested – and Lexon will serve multiple blockchain platforms as target. Currently Ethereum and the Aeternity blockchain are supported. Different *jurisdictions* may be catered to, using programming principles called *librar-ies* and *frameworks*. Transcending its origins, Lexon helps both in many situations that have nothing to do with blockchain – as 'normal' stand-alone program – as well as for applications where legal aspects may be less important, which are inter-ested instead in the raw inclusive power of readable code.

Throughout, special value accrues from how Lexon can capture and process the 'meaning' of a text (pg. 95) across dif-ferent (human) input and (computer) output languages. It can be used to *analyze* a document in different ways. It can also be used to *generate* more powerful user interfaces to manage and interact with the programs and app backends driven by Lexon code. It will allow for automated *testing*, applying existing tools that are used to find program errors to legal agreements (pg. 101). And it will allow to come to fast and error-free eco-nomic judgements about the *value* of a contract (pg. 160).

Collapsing Two Worlds

The list of possible applications for Lexon is long and diverse (pg. 161). It contains private contracting, Decentralized Auton-omous Organizations (DAOs), robotics, trade, law, (ex-ante) regulation, governance, regTech, terms of service, bills of ex-change, financial instruments, provenance, academic certifica-tion, supply-chain, logistics and ride sharing, future proofing of blockchain projects, escrow solutions, wills, crowdfunding, mu-tual and retail insurance, self-sovereign information sale and sharing, and markets for digital assets.

The scope of Lexon's usefulness is relatively broad be-cause the principle it implements is simple and new. It collapses the legal and the programming world into one, in a hitherto unexpected way, cancelling out a myriad of procedural steps that had been required in the past to meaningfully connect these two. This can be seen as elimination of *technical debt*. It both obsoletes many tasks and makes new things possible.

The Democratization of Code

The example from Fig 1 is also found at the online editor demo at **http://demo.lexon.tech**. The example has three parties to it so you would be role playing to really test it out. Wearing the Agent's hat, you would see how it takes but a click to eventually facilitate the payout. A contract like this is safe, legally defendable, inexpensive, and the money is transferred within minutes. For more examples, see pg. 40.

Note that Lexon digital contracts have a potential audience a thousand times the size of that of a smart contract written in Solidity. This will push blockchain technology into the mainstream and fuel a cornucopia of innovation. It may also be the answer to the centuries-old riddle how contracts could gainfully be articulated in a more rigorous and mathematical way. But most of all, people asked to enter into such a smart contract or become attached to a DAO built on them, can now read for themselves what the actual agreement is. *Without having to trust the programmers.* This supplies a link that was still missing in the philosophy of decentralization and trustlessness:[13] it democratizes smart contracts beyond developers.

A general counsel can now verify that the terms they advised are really what is expressed in the code of a smart contract, e.g. to double check the compliance of decentralized devices.

DAO communities can now articulate their DAOs such that every member can read them. A single text can double as both the smart contract code and the legal charta that allows the DAO to become a legal person, own assets and shield its members from liability.

---

[13] 'trustless' is what programmers like to call blockchain-technology: it is supposed to mean 'substituting trust', i.e. allowing for transactions to be possible as if there was trust, in situations where there is none.

Society at large can use this language to articulate the
'**Robotic Laws**[14]' that we need to keep machines and services
honest: to set emergency decision rules for self-driving cars or
address the filter bubbles created in social media.

The Escrow Example Explained

The escrow example from pg. 3 consists of four parts:

- **head**
- **definitions**
- **recitals**
- **clauses**

HEAD

LEX Escrow Contract.

The **head** consists of the **LEX** keyword that marks the beginning
of executable code, and the freely given name after this

---

[14] The science fiction author Isaac Asimov's coined the term Robotic Laws in
the 1940s for the science fiction universe over-arching his short stories and
novels. He evolved them over time and showed how easily they can become
self-contradictory or exploitable by a rogue machine. The Laws are so often
quoted and well known in nerd culture that they will have informed many
discussions about real-world, consequential decision-making algorithms.

First Law – A robot may not injure a human being or, through inaction, allow
a human being to come to harm.

Second Law – A robot must obey the orders given it by human beings except
where such orders would conflict with the First Law.

Third Law – A robot must protect its own existence as long as such protection does not conflict with the First or Second Laws.

Isaac Asimov, 1950: I, Robot; pg. 40.

More on the laws: http://self.gutenberg.org/article/WHEBN0000060136/
Three%20Laws%20of%20Robotics

keyword (in this case **Escrow Contract**) that identifies this contract for filing and maintenance purposes. There can be more information spelled out in the head, such as a revision number and a preamble, or a comment.

To have a *keyword* like **LEX** is useful also for the legal perspective of a digital contract. In the case that the Lexon code is embedded, e.g. as schedule of a larger master agreement, it provides a clear separation between the automated parts and the legal prose that might precede it. Because of this keyword, **LEX**, Lexon digital contracts are NOT entirely seamlessly embedded in the larger document prose that may surround them. But if push comes to shove, a judge would at any rate never be completely ignorant of the fact that there is automation in play with a digital contract. Therefore, it will only help to have a clear indication of where the text relevant for automation starts, to reduce legal attack vectors.

An optional **LEXON** tag can occupy the next line. If it exists, it is followed by a version number that indicates with which version of Lexon the code will work. This is a concession to the fact that Lexon is software and evolving at a rapid pace. Like the name after LEX, this number simply helps keeping order.

A **PREAMBLE** is also optional. This keyword is followed by a high-level description of the contract. In legalese, the 'preamble' is the introduction to a contract that gives context and motivation but is itself not legally binding text. In Lexon, this text is neither legally binding nor part of the automation.

Such an extended head could look like this:

```
LEX Escrow Contract.
LEXON 0.2
PREAMBLE: This is a simple digital contract example.
```

DEFINITIONS

"Payer" is a person.
"Payee" is a person.
"Agent" is a person.
"Fee" is an amount.

Definitions are next. They are similar to what lawyers are used to from normal contracts – and which programmers know as *type declarations*. Because this code example is really a *template* – i.e. not a concrete instance of a concrete agreement yet – the concrete name, address, or blockchain address are not yet known at the time of writing.[15]

Lawyers know the principle of copy-paste well, re-using contracts that have been written for one client for a different client at a later point in time. In a similar fashion, any digital contract, before it is deployed, really defines an entire *class* of possible look-alike contracts.

When a digital contract is deployed, made concrete, the real names and blockchain addresses are provided.

RECITALS

The Payer pays an Amount into escrow, appoints the Payee, appoints the Agent, and also fixes the Fee.

The **Recital**[16] of a digital contract is code that is performed once at the very beginning, before any clause can be executed.

---

[15] Also, Lexon is still in flux and lines like these will look different soon, more like one is used from contract templates in textbooks or on the Internet.

[16] In US law, the recital is the part of a contract that states the purpose of the agreement. It is intended to help interpreting the agreement. In the

This example is simplistic in that the payer sets it all up.

In a traditionally written contract, recitals list the actions taken that led the parties to enter into the agreement. Lexon recitals are similar in that they provide the prerequisite foundation for the clauses that follow. They are performed when the smart contract is signed by the creator and deployed to the blockchain.

CLAUSES

CLAUSE: Pay Out.
The Agent may pay from escrow the Fee to themselves, and afterwards pay the remainder of the escrow to the Payee.

CLAUSE: Pay Back.
The Agent may pay from escrow the Fee to themselves, and afterwards return the remainder of the escrow to the Payer.

The last part here are the **clauses** that define possible outcomes. Payment is exclusively conditional on action of the *Agent* here and can only go to the *Payee* or back to the *Payer*.

European Union, a recital is the part of a law that describes its motivation, ideally free from jargon and politics.

Online Editor and Deployment

Lexon can be tested live, and code can be deployed to a blockchain, directly to Ethereum or Aeternity, at:

> ## http://demo.lexon.tech

The online editor has more documented examples.

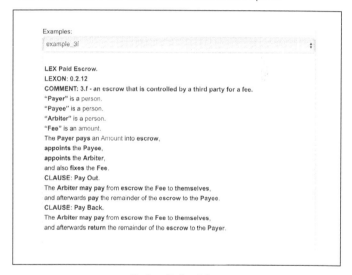

Fig 3 — Online Editor

This is the fastest way to deploy an actual smart contract to a blockchain because it covers all the way from writing Lexon to getting it live and using it: the online editor automatically executes the necessary steps that come after the Lexon compiler did its job.

One can also use the Lexon compiler stand-alone. In this case you would take care of the rest, e.g. to compile and deploy Solidity (pg. 363). The compiler can also be built into any web page (see

Solidity Output

The listing in Fig 4 shows how smart contracts had to be written before Lexon.

No judge would look at this,[17] and proposing such code as contract would trigger a costly battle of experts in court.

Note that the language shown, Solidity, is deemed an *easy* language by programmers but errors made using this language have derailed startups and sunk upward of USD 100,000,000 in funds.[18] The looks of the language, and its relative accessibility have been taken from JavaScript, the language of choice for programming webpages. The rational was that a familiar-looking language would help the adoption of Ethereum. But a pixel hiccup in your webpage is a different story than a glitch in your banking system and traditionally, different languages had been used for programming financial services. Because the blockchain world had created billions in funds the losses went mostly unnoticed outside the bubble. Of course, in the real world, errors like this destroy companies, ruin carriers and put people in the dock. It would seem that lack of readability, even for programmers, might constitute a barrier to adoption for blockchain technology.

Technically, Lexon creates this Solidity code (Fig 4) from the human-readable code above (Fig 1), to satisfy the form that Ethereum needs. The Solidity code is then compiled again, to the (yet less readable) bits and bytes that are actually stored on the Ethereum blockchain. But this is of no concern to a user of Lexon.

---

[17] Listening to a panel of judges commenting on blockchain at Stetson was a key moment to motivate Lexon. They stated convincingly, and not without humor, how they would never, ever look at smart contract code. They would avoid it by every procedural means available, they said, and as last resort call in IT experts to give their opinion but would not touch it themselves. Stetson University College of Law has been ranked #1 in trial advocacy.

[18] https://blog.comae.io/the-280m-ethereums-bug-f28e5de43513

```
pragma solidity ^0.5.0;

contract Escrow {
    address payable payer;
    address payable payee;
    address payable agent;
    uint fee;

    constructor(address payable _payee,
      address payable _agent, uint _fee)
      public {
        payer=msg.sender;
        payee=_payee;
        agent=_agent
        fee=_fee;
    }

    function PayOut() public {
        require(msg.sender == agent);
        arbiter.transfer(fee);
        payee.transfer(address(this).balance);
    }

    function PayBack() public {
        require(msg.sender == agent);
        arbiter.transfer(fee);
        payer.transfer(address(this).balance);
    }
}
```

Fig 4 – Escrow Example: Solidity Output

The Solidity output that Lexon creates will change over time, away from the clean look that serves demonstration today.

There is Solidity code of a similar example that was *not* generated but created by a third party from pg. 367.

Taxonomy

If we call a program running on a blockchain a 'smart contract', and the contract as lawyers know it 'legally enforceable contract' then we have three cardinal relationships that should be differentiated:[19]

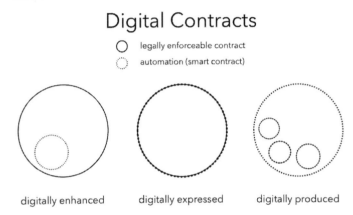

Digital Contracts

○ legally enforceable contract

⊙ automation (smart contract)

digitally enhanced | digitally expressed | digitally produced

Digitally enhanced: a legally enforceable contract is <u>in part</u> automated by a smart contract. The legally enforceable contract 'includes' the smart contract and conventional prose spells out parts that are outside the scope of the smart contract.

Digitally expressed: the smart contract <u>is</u> the legally enforceable contract. The code of the smart contract is the entire text of the legally enforceable contract. This becomes possible through the use of the Lexon language.

Digitally produced: a smart contract running on the blockchain initiates a <u>multitude</u> of legally enforceable contracts, one with each person interacting with the smart contract, which we will call a **Contract Factory**. This is a common pattern that holds e.g. for a crowdfunding smart contract.

---

[19] This graphic & pg. 20 - 22 are in the public domain. H. Diedrich, C. Reyes.

In short:

digitally enhanced	→ the program is a part of a contract.
digitally expressed	→ program and contract are the same.
digitally produced	→ the program produces contracts.

There are nuances and overlaps but it is important to note that smart contracts and legally enforceable contracts are neither necessarily the same nor necessarily two different documents.

Digital Enhancement

The typical 'Ricardian Contract'[20] setup joins traditional contract prose with a blockchain smart contract, e.g. written in Ethereum's Solidity and thus not readable for non-programmers. In this way, human-readable prose is joined with a blockchain component that will automatically perform part of the agreement. An example could be a loan with collateral where the exact conditions of the contract are laid out in the traditional contract's prose, while the payments due for repayment are calculated by a smart contract and automatically deducted from the lender's Ether[21] account. The off-chain prose might deal with exceptions e.g. the case that the lender stops access to his account. This constellation then is what we call *digital enhancement*. Lexon code can be used for these situations, too. And in fact, we predict that it will replace Solidity for most such cases because it will have strong upsides to do so.

Digitally Expressed

But the novelty with Lexon is that the legal contract prose can now itself be the program that is executed on the blockchain.

---

[20] *Ian Grigg*, 1996 – https://en.wikipedia.org/wiki/Ricardian_contract
[21] *Ether* is the name of the crypto currency of the Ethereum blockchain.

Program and contract can virtually be the same as can be observed in the example on pg. 3 where a simple escrow agreement is articulated in Lexon, with the document serving the dual purpose of expressing the 'meeting of the minds' on the one hand but being a program on the other, ready for deployment to the blockchain as is. We call this *digitally expressed*, because there is now only one document that serves as legally enforceable contract that one would show to a judge if needed, and doubles as program on the blockchain.

Digitally Produced & Contract Factory

Very often, however, Lexon code will be used to program a system that offers multiple individuals to enter into contracts, which are each created ad hoc, e.g. at the time a prospect signs off on a purchase, or a membership in a DAO. In this case, one smart contract results into multiple legal agreements. A useful example for this pattern is a ticket vending machine: such a machine can extend an offer to potential buyers of a ticket, e.g. for public transport. When a buyer puts money into the machine it will 'decide' whether to issue the ticket or not. The money has to be enough, the machine needs to check some other conditions, e.g. whether it still has enough paper to print on. Likewise, a smart contract always has the 'last word' whether it will initiate an agreement based on the user input, or not. It can send money back that was sent to it if a condition is not met as needed. The money might be too little, or the deadline or a ceiling for a crowdfunding drive might have been passed. If all is good, the smart contract will accept the offer of the user and a legal agreement commences, usually between the user and the creator of the smart contract. The result is a set of many individual cookie cutter contracts e.g. between many buyers and one seller. We want to call smart contracts that act like this *Contract Factories* – borrowing from a well-known pattern name in computer sciences – and the individual legally enforceable contracts *digitally produced*.

Human-Readability

"I am surprised new languages have not made more progress in simplifying programming."

Bill Gates[22]

The example from pg. 3 displays three distinct aspects of human-readability:

❶ the vocabulary,

❷ the grammar and

❸ the document structure.

In all three categories, there are similarities but also marked differences between legally enforceable contracts and smart contracts – i.e. between prose documents for human consumption and programs. It is this gap that Lexon bridges, in all three aspects.

On this premise rests the claim that Lexon constitutes a new generation [23] of programming languages: all prior

---

[22] https://www.reddit.com/r/IAmA/comments/18bhme/im_bill_gates_co-chair_of_the_bill_melinda_gates/c8dcvve/

[23] Program language generations are loosely defined by how highly they abstract, and how close they get to human thought, making each next generation easier to use, and capable to write more powerful programs in less lines of code. The 1st generation is pure machine code, consisting exclusively of numbers. The 2nd generation assigns abbreviations or even entire words to these numbers (pg. 148). The 3rd generation introduces structure, in the form of loops, if-else-branches, lists and arrays. The 4th generation allows to describe the desired result, somewhat closer to business language, rather than the way there. SQL (pg. 152) is an example. This also includes visual programming tools. The 5th generation arrives at pure mathematical logic striving to leave any notion of program flow behind but consisting instead of rules without any inherent order, like a math formula. This generation was expected to produce AI and programs that would write themselves. Prolog (pg. 78) is an important example.

programming languages have yielded to the *demands of the machine* on their deepest level and to this end all invented something *new* – new vocabulary, new grammar, new document structures – to start out closer to what a machine can understand. Lexon defies conventions in *not* doing that. Its design is based on limitation instead.

Lexon Inverses the Language Design Approach

Lexon starts from the rather complex and irregular realities of natural language vocabulary and grammar. It reduces from there towards a manageable rule set, instead of building a new one from scratch. But Lexon has been created using the same tools that are used to implement today's mainstream programming languages.

The reason this works is that the *models* underlying these tools come from linguistics and were originally designed to reason about *natural* languages. But in the tradition of logicians, the craft of programming language design accepted the premise that inventing new and presumably more powerful symbols was its very core. At the same time, the productivity of the field has also slowed down significantly, which made Bill Gates wonder out loud why there is virtually no progress.[24]

Decades ago, limits of hardware performance made the design trajectory away from natural language necessary and justified it. But this is no longer the case. Arguably, forcing the mind of the programmer to follow the requirements of the computer as prerequisite in the process of coding, could today

---

[24] There is progress, Rust is amazing. But Gates always cared about accessibility and purposefully realized global computer literacy with Office macros.

be questioned as an example of the mortal sin of programming: *premature optimization.*[25]

One could argue the provocative view that Lexon addresses a severe flaw of basically all existing programming languages used in mainstream, professional software development.

And in fact, Lexon code turns out to be exceptionally easy to debug. Because finding errors does become easier for anyone when Wernicke's area can be used for it – the part of the brain that we use to parse language in conversation. Anything that doesn't sound right is probably a bug.[26] This is really different. Human-readability might be for programmers, too.

---

[25] "Premature optimization is the root of all evil," programmers like to say. It is in fact essential to know when and what to optimize to end up on budget and with maintainable code. The natural inclination of programmers is to optimize as much and as early as possible.

[26] As a programmer, you have to see it to believe it. There is a notable speed up when double checking even compared to languages you know very well.

Natural Language Programming

Numerous projects (pg. 323) have in the past proposed program code that reads like human language. But almost universally, they stayed with a 3rd or 4th language generation perspective, i.e. focused on the description of algorithms and data. The more radical ideas didn't get far. The mainstream languages COBOL (1959) and SQL (1974) borrowed from English with intent but remain at a formulaic level and use natural language more as a learning aid and window dressing for the very machine-friendly and mathematical semantics underneath.[27]

The idea to make programs easier to understand by using natural language dates back to the beginning of commercial programming, to Grace Hopper's FLOW-MATIC[28] (1955). The arguments she made[29] were identical to the argument for Lexon, except that she and her colleagues were content to use English to better express low-level *flow charts* – including self-modifying operations. The modest goal then was to overcome the scourge of having to calculate in non-decimal numbers.

But it was a big step forward and FLOW-MATIC's heir, COBOL, took a cue. COBOL is often cited as a cautionary tale to not even think about bringing more of natural language into a programming language. Of course, nobody actually knows COBOL and it's funny because COBOL is a computer language still in mainstream use after an unbelievable 60 years. This doesn't necessarily make for a convincing negative example, much to the contrary, as 60 years in IT is an eternity.

On the other hand, there are program languages

---

[27] For code examples see pgs. 301 and 303 respectively.

[28] For a code example see pg. 299.

[29] https://archive.computerhistory.org/resources/text/Remington_Rand/Univac.Flowmatic.1957.102646140.pdf

specifically made to describe legal contracts, among them the one in Nick Szabo's '94 paper in which he coined the term *smart contracts*.[30] His proposal illustrates that the ambition to create a language for contracts does not have to go hand in hand with the intent to make the language inviting for non-programmers. Szabo focus was on eliminating ambiguity. When the term *smart contracts* later got adopted by the Ethereum developers, they meant to highlight how Ethereum code was unbreakable. In both instances, the notion that contracts should be readable for normal people did not figure.

Likewise, there are many claims today about 'human-readability' for various smart contract languages, but invariably they propose a completely different, more abstract idea than Lexon of what 'human-readable' should mean. They all very much look exactly like program languages, often more like the less mainstream ones, like Lisp or Prolog. In those cases, 'human-readability' may sometimes serve as a pro-active defense against the complaint that they look unfamiliar (e.g. Lisp-like) even for many programmers.

But at least since 2016, everyone in the blockchain scene seemed to feel that it would be a great idea to have smart contracts that would be readable like normal, plain English contracts. Different approaches were tried and it wasn't clear to everyone how far beyond the blockchain the impact of such a new programming language could reverberate.

---

[30] Ibid.

THE
LANGUAGE

Lexon code is optimized for reading,[31] Because programs, as well as contracts, are usually more often read than written, and usually are read by more people than there are writers.

It's an open question right now, how difficult writing Lexon might be, although there are very encouraging examples being created by the community.[32]

What follows is the explanation of the basics of the language that have helped others to get started. We'll first give an impression of how the vocabulary works, then look at how Lexon code is structured, i.e. its 'grammar.'[33]

The grammar is the main focus of the Tutorial chapter from page 39 and the vocabulary is listed in full in the Language Reference from page 177.

---

[31] At the right insistence of Brian J. Fox, creator of bash – a program virtually every programmer has used – and one of the earliest GNU hackers.

[32] The most astonishing contribution, the UCC financing form by Carla Reyes, is presented from pg. 61.

[33] You'll benefit from making sure to get the most up-to-date information but the gist of it as described here will remain the same.

Vocabulary

Lexon's *base* vocabulary at this point is roughly 130 words and word combinations. This is comparable to other mainstream programming languages. The core vocabulary of natural English is estimated to be 850 words (pg. 351).

Off the bat Lexon's expressiveness is much *lower* than what can be said using 850 words in natural language, mainly because it has a very limited number of *verbs*.

But Lexon's base vocabulary can be amended by any number of freely definable *names*, nouns usually, that are used to designate *subjects*, *objects* and *clauses* (!). In the above examples, "**Payer**", "**Payee**", "**Agent**" but also "**Fee**" are such names, as well as "**Pay Out**" and "**Pay Back.**"

Names can consist of multiple words, i.e. include spaces. Clauses are often named for partial sentences, e.g. "**Service Performed as Agreed**," so that they can organically be built into other sentences.[34] This is a major pillar on which Lexon's readability rests. Within those names, no restrictions apply. The effective vocabulary across Lexon contracts is therefore of unlimited size.

To get an idea, here are the words and low-level sentence structures that Lexon recognizes.[35] The words listed can be used as *part* of *names*. Case does not matter. Some words, e.g. articles, are recognized in order *to be ignored*:

---

[34] ☺

[35] As Lexon is in early development, this is a shifting target. The list is based on the source of Lexon 0.2.

a, aborted, after, afterwards, also, amount, amount of, and, and also, and with this, any, anyone, appoint, at all times provided, at any time, at least, be, be made, before or on, being, being on record, binary, burn, calculate, certify, clause, collect, comment, consider, contracts, count of, current, current time, data, date, day, decrease, decreased by, deem, define, difference, divided by, dividing, duration, enter, escrow, fifth, fix, for all, fourth, further in the future than, given, greater or equal to, greater than, half, having been, if … then: … else:, in, in any case, increase, increased by, invoke, is, lesser or equal to, lesser than, lex, lexon, make a payment, may, minus, must, never, no, no-one, not, not the case, notify, now, number of, number of days, offer, on, or, paid, passed, past, pay .. to, person, plus, power of, previous, prior, product of … and, provided, publish, record, recorded value, redefine, remainder, resulting, return, reveal, revoke, seconds, section, send a notification, subtract from, sum of, tenth, terminate, terminate all contracts, terms, text, the, themselves, then, there is, thereby, third, this, this contract, time, time passed since, times, to, token type, Transfer, undefined, whole number, with, yes

Fig 5 – Lexon Base Vocabulary (verbs and compound expressions)

Names

Changing the definition names does not change the logic of the contract.

> LEX Payment.
>
> "Payer" is a person.
> "Payee" is a person.
> "Payment" is an amount.
>
> The Payer pays a Payment to the Payee.

This is a payment, nothing more. The Payer pays an amount to the Payee. This is not even 'really' a contract, because it is so simple.

> LEX Transfer.
>
> **"Sender"** is a person.
> **"Receiver"** is a person.
> **"Sum"** is an amount.
>
> The Sender pays a Sum to the Receiver.

This is the same contract as above, just spelled out using different names. When this contract is signed and deployed to a blockchain, the persons named will have to be named with their real names or at least a blockchain address, to clearly identify them.

That comes later though. At the time of writing, this document is a template and the names defined in it are placeholders. Are that is known is that they must be a person or an amount.

Synonyms

If you use a synonym verb, it does not change the logic of the contract.

LEX Transfer.

"Sender" is a person.
"Receiver" is a person.
"Sum" is an amount.

The Sender **transfers** a Sum to the Receiver.

This is the same contract as the previous one, just spelled out using a different *verb* with the same meaning: **transfer** instead of **pay**.

Note that the verbs in Lexon are predefined and few. You cannot just invent them as with the names (nouns). I.e. the names 'Sender', 'Receiver', and 'Sum' can be replaced by almost any other words you can come up with. But for 'pay' the synonyms are precisely 'transfer' and 'return.' No other words will work.

This is a fundamental difference between nouns and verbs in Lexon. Nouns can be chosen freely, verbs need to be used as intended, looked up in examples or the reference to see what will work.

Neutral Names

LEX Transfer.

"**A**" is a person.
"**B**" is a person.
"**C**" is an amount.

A transfers C to B.

This is the same contract as the previous one, just reducing the definitions to neutral one-letter names.

Articles

Articles (a, an, the) can be left out.

LEX Payment.

"**Payer**" is person.
"**Payee**" is person.
"**Payment**" is amount.

Payer pays Payment to Payee.

Articles and some other words in Lexon are called 'fillers'. They have a big role in making a text easy to read for a human being but are irrelevant to the automation of the contract on the blockchain. Obviously, articles can fundamentally change the meaning of a contract to the human reader. It's on the writer to not abuse them. Reining in the possibilities for abuse of fill words is a high priority for future Lexon tools (cf. pg. 39).

Sentence Grammar

Lexon's basic sentence grammar follows that of English, requiring, in this order: *subject*, *verb*, *object*. Verb and object are grouped together as *predicate*.

In the boxes below, square brackets [ ] mean *'optional'* and the ellipsis ... means *'potentially more of the same'*.

Sentence ⟶ **Subject + Predicate [, Predicate ...]**

Predicate ⟶ **Verb + [Object]**

Fig 6 – Lexon Sentence Rule

These sentences are the main carrier of information in Lexon code. They form the body of **RECITALS** and **CLAUSES**.

The choice of verbs in Lexon is very restricted, while subject and object can each be any blockchain addresses – or legal person for that matter. Within a Lexon contract they will be given an arbitrary name alluding to its function (e.g. **Payer**), which adds meaning for the reader.

The freedom to name variables any way you want is a trait Lexon shares with all modern programming languages. Lexon goes further towards readability by not requiring any artificial style, like Camel Case or Snake Case.[36] It also allows spaces as part of the names, which enhances readability markedly.

Lexon also knows a number of passive constructs that operate on any given subject, e.g.: something **is certified**.

---

[36] Originally as convention, the style of writing variable names: e.g. as **firstName** (Camel Case) or **first_name** (Snake Case). The intent is to leave out spaces. Lexon allows to write: **First Name**.

Document Structure

Technically, the Lexon *document structure* is part of its '*grammar*', because that's how computer languages are defined. This concerns everything beyond those parts that are corollaries of natural language grammar. There is no such thing as a document structure in natural language, but there is in both contracting and programming.

On the highest level, the Lexon code can be embedded into legal contract prose. *Within* the Lexon parts then, the basic structure is:

Head + Definitions + Recitals + Clauses

Fig 7 – Lexon Simple Document Rule

The above rule can also be expressed visually as follows:

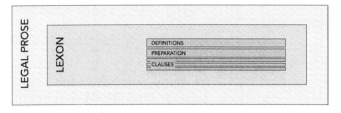

Fig 8 – Lexon Simple Document Rule (graphical)

A minimal contract can be very short and only needs to have the **HEAD** and one sentence of **RECITAL** – or instead of a recital at least one **CLAUSE**.

However, as spelled out below, more complex **Contract Factories** (pg. 20) will see the pattern of **head, definitions, recital, clauses** repeated multiple times over: first within a section called **TERMS**, then within one or more **CONTRACTS** sections.

The **TERMS** define all aspects that are true for the entire digital contract code. The **CONTRACTS** describe individual agreements between only two parties. If more than one type of such agreement is part of the system, there will be as many **CONTRACTS** sections.

Lexon → Head + Terms + Contracts

Terms → Head + Definitions + Recitals + Clauses

Contract → Head + Definitions + Recitals + Clauses

Fig 9 – Lexon Complete Document Rules

The above rule can be visualized as follows:

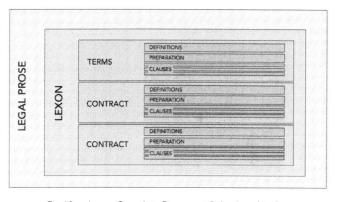

Fig 10 – Lexon Complete Document Rules (graphical)

Most elements given above are optional. Many digital contracts will be simple. This structure is anything but random though and carries the more complex ones.

Within the individual **CLAUSES**, the pattern is:[37]

> **Clause ⟶ Head + Definitions + Permissions +
> Conditions + Statements.**

Fig 11 — Lexon Clause Rule

The above rule can also be expressed visually as follows:

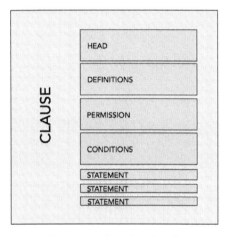

Fig 12 — Lexon Clause Rule (graphical)

Beyond these rules, some terms in the Lexon vocabulary are irregular and have to be learned for each individual term in the vocabulary. They are not used in surprising ways, but cannot be described by a pattern and sometimes cannot be used in all ways that natural English would allow for.

---

[37] This is due to change in the next version of Lexon.

The Double Edge of Language

A caveat: there is nothing in the language itself that keeps the writer from using misleading definitions. Language is not the right level to prevent fraud. Content checks are always one level above language.

```
LEX Payment.

"Payee" is person.
"Payer" is person.
"Payment" is amount.

Payee pays Payment to Payer.
```

The non-sensical swap of **Payer** and **Payee** in this example will confuse readers but the automation of the contract will still work the same as in the examples before. The logical meaning of this code is identical to the one shown before. It is just the labels that are misleading. But it is misleading only to humans since the blockchain virtual machine does not understand the word 'Payer' or 'Payee' at any rate. It does not even get to see them. It just understands what the action 'pay' is.

Lexon is not the promise – at all – that smart contracts *cannot* be misleading. Lexon is the promise that smart contracts *can* be readable. And this example is only a mild instance from a wide spectrum of possible criminal abuse. Unfortunately, there are more powerful ways to make Lexon contracts be as corrupt as bad contracts in other blockchain languages: cleverly misleading definitions, convoluted text, intentional off-by-ones. But ultimately, there is no way for a technical tool to understand if even a completely *correct* contract proposes a completely fraudulent deal.

Allowing for readability is Lexon's first goal. Curbing opportunity for abuse through smart tools will be a continuous task. But note that it is only thanks to the high readability of Lexon that this question comes up in the first place. It would simply not be asked of other blockchain languages.

A judge may throw this contract out because it is going to be difficult to argue that switching the words Payer and Payee was intentional and served a purpose that both sides agreed upon. The contract will still execute 'correctly' on the blockchain, which is the reason why a future version of Lexon will have an option for a judge or arbiter who has been given forum powers to reverse a smart contract with minimal overhead and no consequences for other users of the blockchain that the contract runs on.

You get the basic idea at this point and might consider to check out online resources and cherry pick across the rest of the book. The online editor at **http://demo.lexon.tech** is a great place to get your own first digital contract deployed you will soon be able to actually use it for work.

Next up is a tutorial that steps through small pieces of example code, to show how the theory is applied to practice.

If you don't feel like learning to code at this point, skip forward to the real-world code examples from pg. 40, get philosophical about the meaning of 'meaning' from pg. 142, or go through the domains where Lexon can help from pg. 155,

TUTORIAL

The following is a step-by-step introduction to writing digital contracts that repeats the main learnings up to here and puts them into the context of real code. After completing it, more examples await at **http://demo.lexon.tech** for further study. They are explained in a similar format and you can immediately deploy them to the blockchain.

The basic tenets presented here will hold for 2020 but an updated and enhanced version of this tutorial will be online at **http://lexon.tech/tutorial.**

Text marked like this addresses legal professionals.

Text marked like this is written for software developers.

1: Digital Contracts

LEX Managed Escrow.
LEXON: 0.2.22
PREAMBLE: 0.1.b - an escrow contract that is
controlled by a third party.

"Payer" is a person.
"Payee" is a person.
"Agent" is a person.
"Payment" is an amount.

The Payer pays the Payment into escrow,
appoints the Payee,
and appoints the Agent.

CLAUSE: Pay Out.
The Agent may pay the Payment from escrow to the
Payee.

CLAUSE: Pay Back.
The Agent may return the Payment from escrow to the
Payer.

Managed Escrow
A simple escrow contract.
Example for language version: 0.2.22
Lexon Example: 0.a.01 escrow/digital contracts

The code example shown is both a legally enforceable contract and a blockchain smart contract. This is called a Lexon Digital Contract.

> This is a simple escrow contract. It is a contract between a Payer and a Payee, in which a third person, the Agent, will decide where the money goes.

With Lexon, a contract and a program can be the same thing.

Digital Contracts collapse the legal and the programming world. The consequences of this are not always obvious.

On the one hand, this code is admissible in court as the meeting of the minds between two parties. On the other hand, it can be made to automatically, unstoppably and un-tamperably execute on a blockchain. This takes only a few clicks and is a matter of minutes.

Digital Contracts can be read by anyone, without any knowledge about programming. This tutorial is about learning to write them. You find the newest version online at http://lexon.tech/tutorial

For lawyers: Lexon Digital Contracts can be read by a judge, or anyone else, without the help of experts. Importantly, they are readable to the parties entering into the contract. An important motivation for using Lexon to express blockchain smart contracts is to deny the contracting partners a plausible deniability-excuse in case they have second thoughts.

For programmers: Lexon code is parsed and compiled using compiler building tools like Flex, Bison and pest. The grammar is expressed in BNF and PEG.

2: The Point of Lexon

LEX Will.

"Grantor" is a person.
"Heir" is a person.
"Executor" is a person.

The Grantor pays an Amount into escrow,
appoints the Heir,
and also appoints the Executor.

CLAUSE: Execute.
The Executor may
pay the escrow to the Heir.

Will
A minimal will.
Example for language version: 0.2.22
Lexon Example: 0.a.02 escrow/tutorial

> This example shows a minimal will. As a lawyer, you might find issue with it. That's the point with Lexon: that you can, within seconds.

The novelty with Lexon is that computer code can be read by anyone. A great example is the right reaction of lawyers to the code in this example: it is probably wrong in many ways. But the point of Lexon is that lawyers can chime in immediately to discuss how it could be made right.

But also business people, potential customers or business partners will benefit from being able to actually read the smart contract they might be asked to enter into.

The smart contract, as a program that can manage money, will work. The interesting question is, can it be made safer by writing it the right way?

Lexon helps to put the challenges of smart contracts in sharp relief. It helps to get them right - legally as well as logic-wise, because it broadens the scope of who can take part in their verification.

3: The Main Parts

LEX Managed Escrow.
LEXON: 0.2.22
PREAMBLE: 0.1.b - an escrow contract that is
controlled by a third party.
- -

"Payer" is a person.
"Payee" is a person.
"Agent" is a person.
"Payment" is an amount.
- -

The Payer pays the Payment into escrow,
appoints the Payee,
and appoints the Agent.
- -

CLAUSE: Pay Out.
The Agent may pay the Payment from escrow to the
Payee.

CLAUSE: Pay Back.
The Agent may return the Payment from escrow to the
Payer.

Managed Escrow
A typical, brief smart contract
Example for language version: 0.2.22
Lexon Example: 0.a.04 escrow/parts escrow

Lexon Digital Contracts have a document structure that resembles legal contracts.

> The Lexon code shown here is the same escrow contract as before.

Lexon code always starts with a

· **Head** that begins with the keyword LEX, a name, and can have more meta information.

Then follow three main parts:

· **Definitions** that describe the meaning of names as used in the contract.

· **Recitals** that describe what happens when the contract is brought into existence.

· **Clauses** that list the events that the contract covers.

There are more parts in more complex contracts.

Code of Lexon Digital Contracts can be inserted into the prose of traditional contracts.

But it can also stand alone. In this tutorial we will mainly look at stand-alone examples.

> In general, blockchain smart contracts support two distinct situations: as the small, automated part of a larger contract, or as the complete contract for a simple agreement. But as a matter of fact, there are quite complex smart contract programs out there meanwhile and it turns out that a surprising share of traditional contract prose can be 'blockchainyfied' and with this, automated. Lexon increases the scope where blockchain smart contracts can help.

LEX Will.

- -

"Grantor" is a person.
"Heir" is a person.
"Executor" is a person.

- -

The Grantor pays an Amount into escrow,
appoints the Heir,
and also appoints the Executor.

- -

CLAUSE: Execute.
The Executor may
pay the escrow to the Heir.

Will
A simple smart contract will
Example for language version: 0.2.22
Lexon Example: 0.a.05 escrow/parts will

Same parts in a different example:

· **Head** beginning on LEX, followed by a name.

· **Definitions** that define names.

· **Recitals** describing the first things to happen.

· **Clause** - in this case just one.

> Obviously, definitions are type declarations, the recitals are the constructor code and clauses are functions. There are similarities like this throughout the design of the language. It is at heart, but a computer language built upon the same premises and tools as other programming languages.

Let's look at the head.

4: Head

LEX Managed Escrow.
LEXON: 0.2.22
PREAMBLE: An escrow contract that is controlled by a third party.

"Payer" is a person.
"Payee" is a person.
"Agent" is a person.
"Payment" is an amount.

The Payer pays the Payment into escrow,
appoints the Payee,
and appoints the Agent.

CLAUSE: Pay Out.
The Agent may pay the Payment from escrow to the Payee.

CLAUSE: Pay Back.
The Agent may return the Payment from escrow to the Payer.

Managed Escrow
A simple escrow contract
Example for language version: 0.2.22
Lexon Example: 0.a.06 escrow/head

Lexon code always starts with the head.

The Head of a Digital Contract consists of:

1. The **LEX** keyword, followed by the name of the Digital contract. The LEX keyword tells both the computer and a judge that this is the start of the automated parts of a contract. The name can be any sensible name that helps remembering the contents, managing or filing this code.

The head may consist of only the LEX keyword and the name that follows it.

2. The **LEXON** tag is optional. If it exists, it is followed by a version number that indicates with which version of Lexon the code will work. This is a concession to the fact that Lexon is software and developing at a rapid pace. This number establishes the link between the code and the evolution of Lexon it was made for.

3. The **PREAMBLE** is also optional. This keyword is followed by a description of the contract code to follow. This text is neither legally binding nor part of the automation. It should be followed by an empty line for clarity.

> To have a 'keyword' like LEX is useful also for the legal perspective of a Digital Contract. It provides clear separation between the automated parts of a Digital Contract and legal prose (if any) that might preceed it. Because of this keyword requirement, Lexon Digital Contracts are NOT seamlessly embedded in the larger document prose. But a judge would at any rate never be completely ignorant of the fact that there is automation in play with a Digital Contract. Therefore, it will only help to have a clear indication of where the text that is relevant for automation starts.

The definitions follow the head.

5: Definitions

LEX Managed Escrow.
LEXON: 0.2.22
PREAMBLE: 0.1.b - an escrow contract that is
controlled by a third party.

"Payer" is a person.
"Payee" is a person.
"Agent" is a person.
"Payment" is an amount.

The Payer pays the Payment into escrow,
appoints the Payee,
and appoints the Agent.

CLAUSE: Pay Out.
The Agent may pay the Payment from escrow to the
Payee.

CLAUSE: Pay Back.
The Agent may return the Payment from escrow to the
Payer.

Managed Escrow
A simple escrow contract
Example for language version: 0.2.22
Lexon Example: 0.a.07 escrow/definitions

The first thing after the head are the Definitions.

Definitions start with a name followed by 'is a person', 'is an amount' or whatever else can be said about what that name stands for.

Lexon code describes templates.

Because the contract examples we are looking at here are really templates, we do not yet pronounce a concrete amount, nor a concrete street address or blockchain wallet address. Rather, keywords like person, amount, or data are used to give a first indication of what a name will mean. The concrete information will be put into place once the contract is digitally signed and moved towards the blockchain. You enter it, for example, in the online editor after you hit the button that deploys the contract to the blockchain.

Names can be defined as

- person
- amount
- data

Definitions are something lawyers are familiar with. With Lexon, definitions are less concrete than usual because Lexon code at this stage is a template for multiple contracts, rather than one concrete contract.

The definitions evidently use data types:

- person is a blockchain address.

- amount is an integer.

- data is a hash.

Lexon has composite types. They are limited in scope, so that they can be understood rather intuitively by non-programmers. But they make for powerful constructs regardless. More on that later.

6: Recitals

LEX Managed Escrow.
LEXON: 0.2.22
PREAMBLE: An escrow contract that is controlled by a third party.

"Payer" is a person.
"Payee" is a person.
"Agent" is a person.
"Payment" is an amount.

The Payer pays the Payment into escrow,
appoints the Payee,
and appoints the Agent.

CLAUSE: Pay Out.
The Agent may pay the Payment from escrow to the Payee.

CLAUSE: Pay Back.
The Agent may return the Payment from escrow to the Payer.

Managed Escrow
A simple escrow contract
Example for language version: 0.2.22
Lexon Example: 0.a.08 escrow/recitals

The Recitals set up the context for the performance of the contract.

In Lexon, recitals are code that is executed once before any clause is executed.

> In a traditionally written contract, parties commonly use recitals to list the actions taken that led them to enter into the agreement. Lexon recitals are similar in that they provide the prerequisite foundation for the clauses that follow.

Recitals function as constructor code.

The main part of a Digital Contract are the clauses.

7: Clauses

LEX Managed Escrow.
LEXON: 0.2.22
PREAMBLE: An escrow contract that is controlled by a
third party.

"Payer" is a person.
"Payee" is a person.
"Agent" is a person.
"Payment" is an amount.

The Payer pays the Payment into escrow,
appoints the Payee,
and appoints the Agent.

CLAUSE: Pay Out.
The Agent may pay the Payment from escrow to the
Payee.

CLAUSE: Pay Back.
The Agent may return the Payment from escrow to the
Payer.

Managed Escrow
A simple escrow contract
Example for language version: 0.2.22
Lexon Example: 0.a.09 escrow/clauses

The Clauses describe events that can occur during the lifetime of the Digital Contract. They can also be used to provide definitions of arbitrary terms.

Clauses consist of statements that describe what parties to the contract can do.

Note that every clause in a Digital Contract is optional.

Digital Contracts cannot oblige anyone to do anything.

This is because blockchain smart contracts cannot 'reach out' of the blockchain. They can only incentivize parties to the contract by requiring stakes and rewarding actions.

Recitals and Clauses must have a person as an active, acting subject.

For a blockchain smart contract, for anything to happen at all, someone has to 'trigger' it. Therefore, Digital Contracts do not express requirements in the passive tense.

> The fact that blockchain smart contracts require an actor 'for anything to happen' and cannot oblige parties to the contract to anything, forces a shift in the way that lawyers usually write contracts. Playing to the strengths of blockchain smart contracts requires a focus on providing incentives for performance rather than emphasizing legal remedies in the event of a breach.
>
> It does not make Digital Contracts not contracts: but they are based on a specific subset of mechanisms that can be employed in contracts.

Clauses are functionally functions.

Individual statements in a Digital Contract reflect the requirement to have an acting party.

8: Sentences

LEX Managed Escrow.
LEXON: 0.2.22
PREAMBLE: An escrow contract that is controlled by a third party.

"Payer" is a person.
"Payee" is a person.
"Agent" is a person.
"Payment" is an amount.

**The Payer pays the Payment into escrow,
appoints the Payee,
and appoints the Agent.**

CLAUSE: Pay Out.
The Agent may pay the Payment from escrow to the Payee.

CLAUSE: Pay Back.
The Agent may return the Payment from escrow to the Payer.

Managed Escrow
A simple escrow contract
Example for language version: 0.2.22
Lexon Example: 0.a.10 escrow/sentences

Sentences in a Digital Contract have a structure like in natural language They consist of a subject and a predicate.

As the predicate consists of verb and object this makes for the sentence structure of subject-verb-object.

9: Predicates

LEX Managed Escrow.
LEXON: 0.2.22
PREAMBLE: An escrow contract that is controlled by a
third party.

"Payer" is a person.
"Payee" is a person.
"Agent" is a person.
"Payment" is an amount.

The Payer **pays the Payment into escrow,**
appoints the Payee,
and appoints the Agent.

CLAUSE: Pay Out.
The Agent **may pay the Payment from escrow to the**
Payee.

CLAUSE: Pay Back.
The Agent **may return the Payment from escrow to the**
Payer.

Managed Escrow
A simple escrow contract
Example for language version: 0.2.22
Lexon Example: 0.a.11 escrow/predicates

Predicates consist of one or multiple verbs and objects. Predicates also work like in natural language.

Note that Lexon allows for the concatenation of verbs
that belong to the same subject.

10: The word 'may'

LEX Managed Escrow.
LEXON: 0.2.22
PREAMBLE: An escrow contract that is controlled by a
third party.

"Payer" is a person.
"Payee" is a person.
"Agent" is a person.
"Payment" is an amount.

The Payer pays the Payment into escrow,
appoints the Payee,
and appoints the Agent.

CLAUSE: Pay Out.
The Agent **may** pay the Payment from escrow to the
Payee.

CLAUSE: Pay Back.
The Agent **may** return the Payment from escrow to the
Payer.

Managed Escrow
A simple escrow contract
Example for language version: 0.2.22
Lexon Example: 0.a.12 escrow/permission

'May' has a pronounced role in Digital Contracts.

The keyword 'may' controls who can do what with a Digital Contract.

Note that the logic applied in Digital Contracts is otherwise strictly Boolean (i.e. binary: Yes/No) and not Deontic (obligations and permissions: must/must not). May is the cardinal exception to this rule and is used to express permissions regarding the performance of individual clauses of a Digital Contract.

> The term 'may,' in Digital Contracts, gives a party to the contract agency. Only those allowed by a may clause to perform an action, can. In the example above, only the Agent can perform the Pay Out or Pay Back. As seen from the blockchain: if another party tries to perform these clauses, the smart contract will simply cancel the attempt.

The keyword may acts like a guard, or a permission operator to functions. It works like an assertion.

Let's examine a small example in detail.

11: A Simple Example

> **LEX Payment.**
>
> "Payer" is a person.
> "Payee" is a person.
> "Payment" is an amount.
>
> The Payer pays a Payment to the Payee.

Payment
Simple transfer of funds
Example for language version: 0.2.22
Lexon Example: 0.b.1 payment

> This is a payment, without more. The Payer pays an amount to the Payee.

This simple 'contract' has only three parts: the head, consisting only of the line starting on LEX, after that the definitions are given, finally, one recital.

This is not even 'really' a smart contract, because it is so simple. But let's use the simplicity to highlight a couple of things.

LEX is followed by the name you want to give the script, in this example, the word 'Payment'. This name is used to organize code and contracts but does not have any special meaning to the machine.

The next line defines what a "Payer" is supposed to be. In this case, a person. This points to the fact that Lexon contracts are really templates, because a concrete contract would have a concrete name in this place. When a Lexon contract is deployed to the blockchain, what it gets instead is a unique numeric ID that serves the role of a passport number in the blockchain world: it unambiguously defines which person the Payer is.

After the Payer, we also define what the Payee and the Payment are: a person and an amount respectively. When the contract is deployed to the blockchain, those two parameters will also be made concrete.

Finally, there is the heart of the contract, the 'code': in this case it is not conditional - as contracts usually are - but simply money made changing hands. After that happens, the contract terminates.

We will look at two things now that 'do not matter' for Lexon code: automatic *coloring* of the online editor and the actual *names* you define. Names and colors help to make the code easier to read for humans but are both in their way transparent to the machine. The computer does not understand the meaning of the color 'red' or what the word 'Payer' implies.

12: Color Code

In the online tutorial, some code is shown color-coded. This is only to help the reader; it does not affect automation or legal weight.

Red basically marks names that an author of a smart contract invented.

Dark bold marks all keywords that Lexon understands. They make up Lexon's basic vocabulary, currently around 130 words. As you will see, this vocabulary is extended in interesting ways to provide for unlimited expressiveness.

The online tutorial also uses yellow highlights to mark the relevant changes in the source code from one page of this tutorial to the next.

> The colors are only a matter of support while writing code. They do not affect the legal meaning or the machine interpretation of the code. The colors are not 'part' of the document. E.g. they are added on the fly by the online editor when displaying code.

Dark Red marks variable and function names ('names' and 'clauses' but also the name of the entire 'contract' that is defined by the LEX keyword. These are all user-defined.

Black bold marks Lexon keywords that from fixed part of the language grammar: types, 'verbs' and any term - sometimes consisting of multiple words - that the Lexon compiler understands.

Normal weight black are fillers: words that the Lexon compiler ignores, as familiar, e.g. from SQL.

Red marks special use of variables: These occurances of names are unbound and will be bound to parameters of a function (i.e. clause) in the order of appearance. This is a major proposal Lexon makes as per its language design

to arrive at human-readability and it may be a major ob-
stacle for learners as far as writing Lexon code is concerned.

Violet marks an even more expressive use of names:
these are persons and amounts that are bound to values
that traditionally are implicit with method calls in smart
contracts, e.g. Solidity msg.sender.

13: Names

LEX Transfer.

"Sender" is a person.
"Receiver" is a person.
"Sum" is an amount.

The Sender pays a Sum to the Receiver.

Payment
Simple transfer of funds
Example for language version: 0.2.22
Lexon Example: 0.b.3 payment/renamed

This is the same contract as the previous one, just spelled out using different names.

> This code has the same functionality and meaning as the one shown before (←).

If you change the definition names, it does not change the logic of the contract.

When this contract is 'made real', i.e. signed and deployed to a blockchain, the persons named will have to be named with their real names or at least a blockchain address, to clearly identify them. But this document is a template and the 'names' defined in it are placeholders.

> A contract's meaning, of course, does not depend on the names of definitions that you use. Neither does the automated execution 'care', i.e. the blockchain-side of this code.

Note that we are deliberately blurry with the use of the words contract and smart contract at this point. We will be very precise later.

You might know that there is a passionate discussion in the blockchain and the overlapping legal space, whether smart contracts are contracts or smart at all.

The question is misleading. We will learn in a bit that a more complex Lexon smart contract routinely defines multiple legal contracts.

There is a related specialty of Lexon: Synonyms.

14: Synonyms

LEX Transfer.

"Sender" is a person.
"Receiver" is a person.
"Sum" is an amount.

The Sender **transfers** a Sum to the Receiver.

Payment
Simple transfer of funds
Example for language version: 0.2.22
Lexon Example: 0.b.4 payment/synonyms

This is the same contract as the previous one, just spelled out using a different verb with the same meaning: transfer instead of pay.

This code has the same functionality and meaning as the one shown before.

If you use a synonym verb, it does not change the logic of the contract.

Note that the verbs in Lexon are predefined and few. You cannot just invent them as with the names. I.e. the names 'Sender', 'Receiver', and 'Sum' can be replaced by almost any other words you can come up with. But for 'pay' the synonyms are precisely 'transfer' and 'return' and no other words will work.

This is a fundamental difference between nouns and verbs in Lexon. The nouns can be freely chosen. The verbs need to be looked up in examples or the reference to see what will work. We will later see how 'names' can actually amount to half-sentences, which contributes massively to the readability of Lexon code.

The principles used here are simple and few. The list of verbs to learn are also intuitive and few. The learning process is probably different from learning other programming languages and closer to learning a natural language: starting from snippets that work and modifying it in a trial-and-error fashion. The editor always provides instant feedback whether the Lexon code you are trying is correct.

> obviously, a legal contract's meaning can change massively if just a single operative word is changed. We are taking great care to not f* it up. The synonyms - and the fact that they aresynonyms - will be explained in an auto-generated glossary of terms that Lexon can create and that describes the entire vocabulary used in Lexon. The aim remains though that the contracts are clear out of themselves.

One last illustration of the difference between names and verbs in Lexon follows.

15: Meaningless Names

LEX Transfer.

"A" is a person.
"B" is a person.
"C" is an amount.

A transfers C to B.

Payment
Simple transfer of funds
Example for language version: 0.2.22
Lexon Example: 0.b.5 payment/one letter names

This is the same contract as the previous one, just reducing the definitions to be neutral one letter names.

> This code has the same functionality and meaning as the one shown before.

As you see, the names really don't matter. You cannot do this with a verb though. Instead of 'transfers' you could write 'pays' or 'returns' if that makes the contract better readable for human readers.

 This is in keeping with how definitions can be used in legal texts.

There is another change versus the previous example: in the recital 'A transfers C to B.' all articles have been left out.

16: Articles

```
LEX Payment.

"Payer" is person.
"Payee" is person.
"Payment" is amount.

Payer pays Payment to Payee.
```

Payment
Simple transfer of funds
Example for language version: 0.2.22
Lexon Example: 0.b.6 payment/articles

Articles (a, an, the) can be freely used or left out.

> The meaning of the code is identical to the one shown before.

Articles and some other words in Lexon are called 'fillers'. They have a big role in making a text easy to read for a human being but are irrelevant to the automation of the contract on the blockchain.

> Obviously, articles can fundamentally change the meaning of a contract. The writer of a Lexon contract must take care to not abuse them. Reining in the possibilities for abuse of fill words is a high priority for future Lexon tools. But language is not the right level to prevent fraud as it must provide uninhibited expression. Content checks are always one level above language.
>
> Lexon is not the promise - at all - that smart contracts could not be misleading. Lexon is the promise that smart contracts can be readable. The reality is that this is only

the edge of a wide spectrum of criminal intent. Unfortunately, there are more powerful ways to make Lexon contracts be as bad as bad contracts in other blockchain languages: i.e. misleading definitions, convoluted texts, intentional off-by-ones. On the far side of this spectrum, there is no way for technical tools to ever understand if even a completely correct contract proposes a completely fraudulent deal.

Allowing for readability is first. Curbing opportunity for abuse through smart tools will be a continuous task.

Note that thanks to the high readability of Lexon this question comes up in the first place. It would simply not be asked of other blockchain languages.

The get this out of the system, here is an abusive example next.

17: Misleading Names

LEX Payment.

"Payee" is person.
"Payer" is person.
"Payment" is amount.

Payee pays Payment to **Payer**.

Payment
Simple transfer of funds
Example for language version: 0.2.22
Lexon Example: 0.b.7 payment/misleading names

There is nothing in the language itself that keeps you from using misleading definitions. It will confuse readers but the automation of the contract will still work.

> The meaning of this code is identical to the one shown before. It is just the labels that are misleading.

But only to humans since the blockchain does not understand the word 'Payer' or 'Payee' at any rate. It just understands what the action 'pay' is. The rest is implicit.

A judge may throw this contract out because it is going to be hard to argue that switching the words Payer and Payee was intentional and served a purpose that both sides agreed upon regarding the intent of this contract. The contract will still execute 'correctly' on the blockchain, which is the reason why a future version of Lexon will have an option for a judge or arbiter who has been given forum powers to reverse a smart contract with minimal overhead and no consequences for other users of the blockchain that the contract runs on.

18: Meta Information

> LEX Timestamp.
> **LEXON: 0.2.16**
> **COMMENT: 1.a.1 - a timestamp of a data hash**
>
> The "Data" is a data.
> The "Time" is a time.
>
> Data be certified,
> with Time fixed as the current time.

Payment
Simple Timestamping
Example for language version: 0.2.22
Lexon Example: 1.a.1 timestamp/data 1

Two keywords, **LEXON** and **COMMENT** can help working with Lexon code. The information associated with them is not part of the code proper but helps filing, processing and understanding it.

> This contract attaches a timestamp to arbitrary information that will serve to prove that a certain information existed at a certain point in time.

The keyword **LEXON** is followed by a colon and then the compiler and language version number for which the code below it is intended for. In programming, this is a crucial information to avoid errors due to a change in rules. After the **'COMMENT'** keyword, any text may be noted that names or gives context to the understanding of the code below it. Both **LEXON** and **COMMENT** are optional.

Get interactive at **http://demo.lexon.tech**, which has more examples, explained in a similar format, which you can tinker with and immediately deploy to the blockchain.

The newest version of this tutorial also continues online at **http://lexon.tech/tutorial/continue**

We will now turn to three interesting, larger contract examples.

EXAMPLES

The following examples show what Lexon will be able to do and how digital contracts will look in practice. In February 2020 they are work in progress.

First, a preview of how US law might look written in Lexon. This is an actual proposal to the relevant reform committee of the Universal Commercial Code (UCC).

The 'lexonification' of a standard service agreement follows, crafted for the Civil Law jurisdiction of Switzerland (pg. 83).

A pure blockchain play is next, listing the Lexon code for the popular Moloch DAO, a project less concerned about legal fine print (pg. 85).

Note how the examples in this section are digital contracts that attain full identity of program and legal prose. They are *digitally expressed* rather than merely *digitally enhanced* (cf. pg. 20). The Moloch example is *Contract Factory* as it *digitally produces* multiple individual legal agreements.

UCC Financing Statement

The example below[38] is part of a proposal to reform the notice filing system included in Article 9 of the U.S. Uniform Commercial Code (UCC). Specifically, the example is of a smart contract-based UCC-1 form – a financing statement that secured lenders use to notify other prospective lenders that a loan has been made that takes specific assets as collateral.[39] The main function of the UCC-1 financing statement is not in the cryptocurrency aspect. Rather, the key aspect is foremost about record keeping.

This code allows to keep track of the status of the UCC Financing Statement and related collateral in a way that is more powerful than the current implementation in US law. It is expected to better serve the notice function of the Article 9 filing system.

This example represents the Implementation or performance of law, with the understanding that the states' filing offices **can implement law directly on the blockchain.**

This code has **definitions**, a lot of **clauses** and no **recitals**. It is structurally simpler than the escrow contract we looked at before.

---

[38] This discussion of the UCC Financing Statement example is drawn from Carla L. Reyes, *Creating a Crypto-Legal Structure: The UCC Financing Statement* (2019) (unpublished manuscript). For further discussion of the underlying concepts, see Carla L. Reyes, *Conceptualizing Cryptolaw*, 96 NEB. L. REV. 384 (2017).

[39] UCC § 9-502. CONTENTS OF FINANCING STATEMENT – https://www.law.cornell.edu/ucc/9/9-502

LEX: UCC Financing Statement

"Filer" means [a person], with phone number of [phone number] and email of [email].

"Debtor" means [a person's name], known as [Public Key], located at [mailing address, city, state, postal code, country].

"Secured Party" means [a legal person's name], known as [Public Key], located at [mailing address, city, state, postal code, country].

"The Filing Office" means [the name of the state filing office], known as [one public key belonging to the Filing Office].

"Collateral" means [UCC category of collateral], identified by the following number: [hash]

"Digital Asset Collateral" means [an amount].

"Financing Statement Date" means the filing date.

CLAUSE: Lapse Date.
Lapse Date means five years after the Financing Statement Date or five years after the Continuation Statement Date, whichever is later.

CLAUSE: Continuation Window.
Continuation Window means from six month before the Lapse Date to the Lapse Date.

CLAUSE: Reminder Fee.
The Secured Party may pay a Reminder Fee into escrow.

CLAUSE: Notification.
The Filing Office may, at the first day of the Continuation Window, send a Notification Statement to the Secured Party and then pay the Reminder Fee to themselves.

CLAUSE: Notification Statement.
Notification Statement means the text "Your Continuation Statement for [the id of this UCC Financing Statement] is due on or before the [Lapse Date]."

CLAUSE: Continuation Statement.
The Secured Party may during the Continuation Window, certify the Continuation Statement Date to be the current date.

CLAUSE: Termination Statement.
The Secured Party may terminate this UCC Financing Statement.

CLAUSE: Clear.
The Filing Office may terminate this UCC Financing Statement one year after the Lapse Date.

CLAUSE: Pay Escrow In.
The Debtor pays Digital Asset Collateral into escrow.

CLAUSE: Default.
The Secured Party may declare Default.

CLAUSE: Give Possession.
The Filing Office may, upon Default, pay the escrow to the Secured Party.

CLAUSE: Amend Collateral.
The Secured Party may change the Collateral.

CLAUSE: Amend Debtor.
The Secured Party may change the Debtor.

The **Filer** will usually be a bank employee or outside counsel for the bank, the **Debtor** is the person taking out a loan, the **Secured Party** is the bank. The **Collateral** is the real-world object the debtor is putting up as security. It can also be cryptocurrency and similar, i.e. **Digital Asset Collateral.**

The **Reminder Fee** is a fee that the bank can pay to the filing office, but is not required to pay. If the bank pays it, the filing office *may* send a **Notification** to remind the bank to put in a **Continuation Statement** every 5 years – i.e. during the **Continuation Window**. Else, the statement will lapse. Note that while many features of this example merely effect existing rules related to the UCC filing system, this feature of the example represents a new proposal.

That there is no *obligation* described here is in keeping with blockchain powers. A blockchain smart contract cannot coerce anyone to do anything. It can only incentivize.

If the debtor **Defaults**, all that is needed is that the bank says so. This is the intended way the law works, not a weakness introduced by blockchainification. It is clearly an oracle-moment,[40] and a weird one because the bank as **Secured Party** can simply say that the money should now be theirs. This power, however, comes from the underlying contract provisions that are part of the secured loan documentation. The idea of ensuring that the **Filing Office** retains a role in relation to Digital Asset Collateral, in that without its action to **Give Possession** the collateral is not actually going to go to the bank is an attempt to address the unique Issues around custody and priority in the context of Digital Asset Collateral. If the **Collateral** is a real-world item and not **Digital Asset Collateral**, the regular rules related to self-help repossession apply. By law though, the moment the bank says so, they collateral is theirs. If the bank cheats, it's fraud.

Notably, a further feature of this smart contract is that it records exactly who said what when: including that the bank claimed that there was a default as precondition to seizing the assets. This trail of information is what matters.

Proposing law to be written in Lexon is pretty rad. But the next example was equally unexpected in its modest ways.

---

[40] Oracles, in blockchain-speak, are the gates through which facts from the outside world are made known within the confines of the digital blockchain data world.

Service Agreement with Escrow

Lexon can be used to bring normal, legal contracts on-chain. This can be surprisingly useful and elegant. A broad portion of such a contract's text can turn out to be 'more than just prose' and go on the blockchain.

In the example below,[41] Lexon will ignore only the text *in italics* as 'boilerplate,' i.e. as prose that may be necessary for legal purposes or clarity but not for automation. Lexon can tell the boilerplate apart on its own.

The italics are not required to write Lexon code but used here for illustration.

LEX: Service Agreement with Escrow.

PREAMBLE:
A simple service agreement under Swiss law with built-in escrow.

CLAUSE: Offer.
The "Service Provider" pays half of the "Assessment Fee" into escrow, sets the amount of the "Service Fee", sets the "Delivery Time", and also appoints the "Assessor".
By executing all of the above, the Service Provider creates a binding offer.

CLAUSE: Acceptance.
A "Client" pays the Service Fee into escrow, and also pays half of the Assessment Fee into escrow.

The "Due Date" is defined as the duration of Delivery Time after the current time at that point in time.
By executing all of the above, the Client accepts the offer.

---

[41] Courtesy Benedikt Schuppli.

CLAUSE: Provision of Services.
The Assessor may certify either that the "Provision of Services Have Met the Defined Service Criteria" or not, and also certify the "Time of Provision of Services".

CLAUSE: Pay Out.
The Service Provider may, if Time of Provision of Services is certified to be before or on the Due Date, and the Provision of Services Have Met the Defined Service Criteria then pay the Service Fee from escrow to themselves, and also pay the Assessment Fee from escrow to the Assessor.

CLAUSE: Pay Back.
The Client may if the Due Date is past and it is not the case that the Provision of Services Have Met the Defined Service Criteria, then pay the Service Fee from escrow to themselves, and also pay the Assessment Fee from escrow to the Assessor.

GENERAL TERMS:
I. The Service Provider will provide to the Client the Services on or before the Due Date.
II. The Service Provider will provide the Services with the applicable standard of care.
III. Both the Service Provider and the Client will carry their respective tax and applicable levies.

The Moloch DAO

This is an implementation of the Moloch DAO,[42] a minimalist DAO contract, very well known in blockchain-circles that allows members to fund, vote and elect new members in the style of a cooperative. Members can also quit and pull their funds out.

There is no boilerplate in this example. All of the code goes on the blockchain. The example has all four sections described above: head, definitions, recitals, clauses. It also has **CONTRACT** sections[43] that are described further down. Essentially such a section defines a 1:1 relationship between the DAO and a given member. Each **CONTRACT** section exhibits the same structure as the document at large: i.e. head, definitions, recitals, clauses.

LEX MOLOCH.

TERMS:

"Summoner" is [a person].
"Period Duration" is defined as a duration of a fifth of a day.
"Voting Phase Duration" is defined as a duration of 7 days.
"Grace Phase Duration" is defined as a duration of 7 days.
"Abort Window Duration" is defined as a duration of 1 day.
"Proposal Deposit" is [an amount].
"Dilution Bound" is defined as 3.
"Processing Reward" is [an amount].
"Summoning Time" is [a time].
"Approved Token" is [a token].
"Summoner's Initial Number Of Shares" is defined as 1.
"Total Shares" is [an amount].
"Total Shares Request" is [an amount].

---

[42] Solidity source code and explanation at https://github.com/Moloch-Ventures/moloch

[43] The CONTRACT syntax is under revision and will be documented shortly.

The Summoner sets:

the "Approved Token" to any token type;

the "Period Duration" to a duration of time in seconds, greater than 0;

the "Voting Phase Duration" to a duration of time in seconds, greater than 0;

the "Grace Phase Duration" to a duration of time in seconds, greater or equal to 0;

the "Abort Window Duration" to a duration of time in seconds, greater than 0 and lesser or equal to the Voting Phase Duration;

the "Processing Reward" to any amount that is at least 0;

the "Proposal Deposit", an amount that must be greater or equal to the Processing Reward;

the "Dilution Bound", an amount that must be greater than 0.

The "Summoning Time" be defined as the Current Time.

The "Voting Phase Periods" is defined as the whole number resulting from dividing the Voting Phase Duration by the Period Duration.

The "Grace Phase Periods" is defined as the whole number resulting from dividing the Grace Phase Duration by the Period Duration.

The "Abort Window Periods" is defined as the whole number resulting from dividing the Abort Window Duration by the Period Duration.

The Summoner enters into a Member Contract with Summoner's Initial Number Of Shares.

Then, the number of Total Shares is set to the number of the Summoner's Initial Number Of Shares.

CLAUSE: Current Period Number.
The "Current Period Number" is defined as the whole number resulting from calculating the time passed since Summoning Time, divided by the Period Duration.

CONTRACTS per Member:

"Member" is a person.
"Owned Shares" is an amount.
"Proposal Number of Latest Yes Vote" is a number.

The Member is appointed.
The number of Owned Shares is set.

CLAUSE: Eligibility To Ragequit.
Eligibility To Ragequit is defined as Having Never Voted Yes
or the Proposal of the Latest Yes Vote having been Processed.

CLAUSE: Having Never Voted Yes.
"Having Never Voted Yes" is defined as no Latest Yes Vote being on record.

CLAUSE: Rage Quit.
A Member may, if the Member has Eligibility To Ragequit then:
Burn the number of Shares To Be Burned,
and afterwards pay the Rage Compensation for the Shares To Be Burned to themselves.

CLAUSE: Rage Compensation.
The "Rage Compensation" is defined as the amount in escrow times the Burned Shares divided by the sum of the Total Shares and the Burned Shares.

CLAUSE: Burn.
Owned Shares are decreased by the Given Amount.
Total Shares are decreased by the Given Amount.

CONTRACTS per Proposals:

The "Proposer" is a person.
The "Applicant" is a person.
The "Shares Requested" is an amount.
The "Starting Period Number" is a number.
"Yes Votes" is a number.
"No Votes" is a number.
"Processed" is binary.
"Can Pass" is binary.
"Passed" is binary.
"Aborted" is binary.
The "Token Tribute" is an amount.
"Details" is a text.
The "Maximum Total Shares At Yes Vote" is a number.
The "Proposal" is this contract.

CLAUSE: Submit Proposal.
An Applicant may offer a Token Tribute in Approved Tokens,
set the Shares Requested,
set the Details,
and by this Create a Proposal with the Shares Requested.

CLAUSE: Create a Proposal.
The record of the Total Shares Requested be increased by the Shares Requested.

The Proposal Deposit in Approved Tokens be collected from the Proposer to the escrow.
The Token Tribute in Approved Tokens be collected from the Applicant to the escrow.

The "Last Blocked Period Number" be defined as the greater of the Current Period and the Starting Period of the Last Proposal.

The "Starting Period Number" be defined as the Last Blocked Period Number increased by 1.

The "Last Voting Phase Period Number" be defined as the sum of the Starting Period Number and the Voting Phase Duration In Periods minus 1.

The "Last Abort Period Number" be defined as the sum of the Starting Period Number and the Abort Window Periods minus 1.

The "Proposer" is defined as the Member.
The "Applicant" is set.
The "Shares Requested" is set.
The "Token Tribute" is set.
The "Details" are set.

The "Maximum Total Shares" At Yes Vote be recorded as 0.

CLAUSE: Voting Phase Expired.
"Voting Phase Expired" is defined as the Current Period Number being greater than the Last Voting Phase Period Number.

CLAUSE: Abort Window Has Not Passed.
"Abort Window Has Not Passed" be defined as Current Period Number being lesser or equal than Last Abort Period Number.

CLAUSE: Submit Vote.
A Member may certify a Vote.
The Vote must be "yes" or "no".
If the Vote is "yes" then:
Increase the count of Yes Votes by the number of the Shares of the Member,
and also record the Last Vote of the Member,
and also Track Maximum of Total Yes Votes.

Else: increase the count of No Votes by the number of the Shares of the Member.

CLAUSE: Track Maximum of Total Yes Votes.
If the count of Total Shares is greater than the recorded value of Maximum Total Shares At Yes Vote then the recorded value of Maximum Total Shares At Yes Vote be changed at that point to the count of Total Shares.

CLAUSE: Evaluate Proposal.
The Proposal is considered Processed.
Decrease the record of Total Shares Requested by Shares Requested.

If the amount of Yes Votes is greater than the amount of No Votes then the Proposal Can Pass.

If the Dilution Bond is Exceeded then the Proposal Can Not Pass.

If the Proposal Can Pass and the Proposal has not been Aborted then: Pass Proposal;

else: transfer the Token Tribute in Approved Tokens from escrow to Applicant;
Pay the Processing Reward in Approved Token from Escrow to the Executor;
Pay the Proposal Deposit less the Processing Reward in Approved Tokens to the Proposer.

CLAUSE: Dilution Bond is Exceeded.
"Dilution Bond is Exceeded" is defined as the amount of Total Shares times the Dilution Bond being smaller than Max Total Shares At Yes Vote.

CLAUSE: Pass Proposal.
The Proposal is deemed Passed.
If the Applicant is not a Member then, Enlist Applicant as Member.

Increase record of Total Shares by the number of Shares Requested.
Transfer the Token Tribute in Approved Tokens from escrow to Guild Bank.

CLAUSE: Abort.
The Applicant may, if the Abort Window Has Not Passed then Pull Out.

CLAUSE: Pull Out.
The amount of Tokens To Abort be defined as the amount of the Token Tribute,
afterwards, Token Tribute be changed to 0,
and with this, the Proposal is Aborted,
afterwards, Transfer the Tokens To Abort to the Applicant.

CLAUSE: Member Proposal Vote.
Reveal Vote Of Member.

The logic of the original Moloch DAO, as proposed by its creators using Solidity, is somewhat obscured by technicalities like the voting *periods* and the way that adding members and voting on proposals are rolled into one.

A couple of notes for astute readers:

Abort Window Has Not Passed is an expression that is defined by being the *name* of a clause:

CLAUSE: Abort Window Has Not Passed.
"Abort Window Has Not Passed" be defined as Current Period Number being lesser or equal than Last Abort Period Number.

… and is then *used as part of a sentence*, just like a definition in a legal contract would. A programmer, of course, would call this, a *function*.

> The Applicant may, if the **Abort Window Has Not Passed** then Pull Out.

The Same reason is behind the various upper-case spellings throughout the document, e.g.:

> If the **Dilution Bond is Exceeded**, then the Proposal Can Not Pass.

> The amount of **Tokens To Abort** be defined as the amount of the Token Tribute.

… all these occasions are (multi-word) definitions, i.e. names of CLAUSES, and as such need to be included into the prose exactly as defined as CLAUSE name.

And it is the reason for the wooden wording of:

> The Applicant may, if the **Abort Window Has Not Passed** then Pull Out.

… as **"Abort Window Has Not Passed"** is a fix phrase that is chosen freely and as pragmatically as possible but, in the end, needs to work as both the name of a **CLAUSE** and as part of a sentence.

By the same token*, it is not allowable to insert "by" between **Aborted** and **then** to make this sentence prettier:

> If the Proposal Can Pass and the Proposal has not been Aborted then: Pass Proposal;

Because the **then** is a part of the **if** construct that this sentence is. While Lexon has a liberal regimen regarding articles and some other fill words, this is not a place nor a word (i.e. **by**) that is allowable, and this place cannot be made to read better in this way.

The recital of CONTRACTS per Members …

> The Member **is appointed.**
> The number of Owned Shares **is set.**

… operates without active subject. The active party is going to be whoever deploys the smart contract to the blockchain, i.e. signs off on the entire LEX document and puts it into operation. This is not fixed at the time this template code is written. The person will be named the **Summoner** when the deployment happens.

COMPUTATIONAL LAW

> *"While the idea of mechanized legal analysis is not new, its prospects are better than ever due to recent technological developments … Legal technology based on Computational Law has the potential to dramatically change the legal profession, improving the quality and efficiency of legal services and possibly disrupting the way law firms do business. More broadly, the technology has the potential to bring legal understanding and legal tools to everyone in society."*
>
> Michael Genesereth[44]

Lexon may deliver the Holy Grail to Computational Law, providing a way to automate analysis. Computational Law is the study of the 'mechanization' of legal reasoning. It attracts controversy because it calls for rigidity in the specification of laws.

'Mechanized' natural language grammar seems to be the conduit for automating contracts and to achieve 'mechanized' legal analysis. This may conclude a quest of 350 years, which has variously been attacked as too optimistic or suspected to be held back by conspiracy.

That Lexon digital contracts can also reliably self-perform goes beyond the original 1940s vision of Computational Law.

---

[44] Computational Law; at CodeX: The Center for Legal Informatics, Stanford University – http://complaw.stanford.edu/readings/complaw.html

The self-propelled and incorruptible nature of blockchains had not been envisioned. It also goes beyond the early dreams mankind had about computers and robots. Accordingly, thanks to 'trustless' technology, Computational Law looks poised to take on an even more prominent role, reaching beyond simplification to something of a new quality: a reality where it *does* make sense to talk about *facts*, true and false, because the blockchain circumscribes a horizon in which signatures – as expression of will – and money – as carrier of value – exist in an undeniable way. For this to be possible, logic had to come around to embrace induction. Blockchains in this light are to computing what quantum theory signified for physics: the embrace of probability instead of facts.

But Lexon's contribution is on the logical side and the promise of 'mechanized' legal analysis is spectacular enough. From the start, analysis was a major part of the quantum leap that computers seemed to hold for the legal domain. The other being digital search: the revolution in discovery that started in the 1970s. And it may help to imagine how fantastic electronic search must have looked a hundred years ago, to open one's mind to the enormity of change that electronic analysis may bring. It took longer than expected. For it to happen, law had to be re-united with logic.

This may be possible now because 2000 years on, logic has finally caught up with the real-world necessities of the legal profession.

Law currently does not hold itself as a science of logic. Because contrary to intuition, logic as we know it today is not an automatic faculty from birth. It has seen a lot of progress over the last centuries, with the legal profession having material and early influence on it, as well as on the development of programming.

For some this may not make the claim that contracts could or should be written like programs more palatable. In a way the proof is in the pudding, e.g. pg. 83. But it's a legit plausibility check to ask why things should be possible now that ostensibly weren't before. The answer does not lie in the advent of raw computing power, smart text blocks or digital document management. Amazing as they are, they did not make the difference. The answer may instead lie in how the young practice of programming has evolved logic to the degree that it can now be applied to law. Logic might have had to go through the cambric explosion manifest in the millions of professional programmers and billions of lines of code that have sprung into existence over the last decades, before the cross pollination could start. It may only now be powerful enough.

Law and Logic

"The relation between law and logic has been governed, as many of the most intense relationships are, by both a strong attraction and persistent strife."[45]

C. Roversi

While it was a professor of law who first dreamed up a universal formal language and kicked off computer sciences (pg. 110), law seems to have in the meantime developed an allergy against logic. On fair grounds, one could say, as logic was so far behind for so long, in hock of philosophers who were less interested in practical application. But the degree to which law has divorced formal logic may be going a bit far.

There is a lot of benefit to be had from healing this rift. Lexon is obviously an invitation to do that. If in the past it made sense to leave logic behind as it could not bring itself to become consistent and pragmatic, with the advent of higher-order logic and programming that can no longer be said.

---

[45] C.Roversi, 2005: Law and Logic –
https://link.springer.com/chapter/10.1007/1-4020-3505-5_53

Like legal cases, programs are very *real*. Like law, they are rooted in a deductive premise of truth and provability and still have to operate in a world where hard facts are often impossible to come by. Where constant awareness is demanded of the limits of the model of the world that is the subject of a case – or program. Both jurists and programmers have to deliver results and have developed accepted techniques – best-practices at heart – for how to operate under adverse conditions. Namely, with incomplete knowledge.

The intuition might be that it was too abstract a challenge for the legal profession to come up with a math-like, deeply nestable grammar for law, an artificial vernacular with the reasoning powers of a programming language. The inclination to reach straight for Deontic logic (the arithmetic of *shall* and *must not*) instead of Boolean (*true* and *false*) would not have helped[46] (pg. 114). But in reality, it was simply timing: first and higher-order logic, on which programming is based, only arrived now, the result of a major push of mathematicians to clean house a hundred years ago. They did not exist in Antiquity when the foundations of law were laid. It would be an anachronism to fault law for not being based on higher-order logic, or to blame members of the legal profession for being skeptical about it.

Types of Ambiguity

Some of the perceived distance between programming and law is a misunderstanding: programming is 'messier' as it may

---

[46] Boolean logic allows arithmetic of the type $\neg\,\mathbf{A} \wedge \neg\,\mathbf{B} = \neg\,(\mathbf{A} \vee \mathbf{B})$ – read *not A and not B is the same as, not: A or B*. Deontic logic has a problem with this, because roughly put, it is ambiguous what the negation of an obligation is: *not obliged*, or *obliged not to*. This reflects a real problem of real contracts. Lexon *mostly* stays with Boolean truth values as this is the logic that smart contracts know. The word *'may'* has a central role though.

seem, because programs, like laws, live in the real world. And in so far, the concern that a naïve, overly rigid take is proposed is not justified. Programmers are pragmatists, too, and the craft of programming has evolved accordingly.

While many legal practitioners have learned that exactitude is not wanted for law, lawyers versed in blockchain smart contracts appreciate that the term *smart contract* was invented precisely to describe a vision (and a language) [47] to arrive at less ambiguous contracts, without denying that not all outcomes can be addressed up front. Obviously, machines like it crisp. To achieve automation some clarity would be indispensable. But the proposal to reduce ambiguity was never about leaving no questions open. Especially smart contracts leave things TBD all the time, calling lose ends 'oracles.' [48] Smart contract languages have a second mechanism that they share with virtually all mainstream programming languages, which is called 'exceptions.' These are structural facilities built into the deepest layers, which are qualitatively special and exist specifically to allow for the handling of the unforeseen. They acknowledge explicitly that programs and smart contracts serve a world that is not completely predicable and, at least subjectively, non-deterministic.

To some extent, the special sound of 'legalese' is the profession's organic attempt to create a distinct language for law, where certain phrases enjoy unambiguous meaning. That these phrases sound antiquated helps to distinguish the intended meaning from the literal meaning that could be a plausible alternative reading in a given context. This exists, because it is helpful. A program-like language doesn't make that worse it will just sound different. It may allow to be more precise about

---

[47] http://www.fon.hum.uva.nl/rob/Courses/InformationInSpeech/CDROM/Literature/LOTwinterschool2006/szabo.best.vwh.net/contractlanguage.html

[48] Oracles are so central for blockchains that one of the major selling points of Aeternity is that it has a better oracle integration.

what is left open. But it does not require to define every possibly outcome up front.

To the extent that ambiguity is understood as wriggle room for someone to say "you know what, this doesn't make sense" – or, "you know what, 50 bucks and I'll look the other way" – the cold mechanical nature of blockchains is their very contribution. To end this. They will make exchange possible that now can't flourish because people could not be asked to be so heartless – or unselfish – to uphold the required rules while the margins don't have room to pay a policing mechanism.

It would not be the first time that strictness actually empowers human quality to shine as a result, benefitting from and protected by a reliable foundation. *Exceptions* and *oracles* will be used to safeguard against unintended cases of hardship.

As a net effect this might create massive new demand for lawyers as people might contract in situations that today are not seen as important enough to do so, because taking such contracts to court could never be cost-effective. But with smart contracts making enforcement obsolete, because they just can't be broken, the focus shifts from litigation to contract writing. The cost is more predictable, smaller and up front and the upside goes to lawyers instead of attorneys.

This will further be aided by the way that Lexon can help reducing complexity to a degree that might be hard to imagine: *Modularization* is a term from computers sciences that describes how chunks of functionality are compartmentalized into subsections that can be created, understood and tested independently. And that can then be used as building blocks for larger systems. A module is typically of the size that is not too complex to be understood as a whole, in the sense that it is small enough that its logics fits into a human brain all at once. That all its implications and possible exceptions can be surveyed mentally and no surprising emergent behavior should escape the coders. A system composed from such modules would then likewise become easier to understand because the well-defined net functionality of each module is all that needs to be kept present, its finer details are 'encapsulated' and hidden away, on purpose.

Lawyers do this now when crafting complex contract systems that consist of many sub contracts. But they have not arrived at the degree of automation that programmers had to achieve to govern the millions of lines of code and much higher fragility of programs where an error often meant that the entire program will stop. Because different from contracts, computer code is performed down to the last line, again and again, while it is in force. E.g. a computer game that heats up your processor really uses all that processing power for hours on-end to execute billions of instructions a second and if only some of them were wrong, you would see the pixel errors immediately on your screen. An 8-core 3 GHz processor that busies its vents really processes close to a hundred trillion commands an hour. The commands are of a very low machine level but they result from the higher-level code that the programmers wrote, they reflect any error the programmers might have made and there is so much to do because every last detail of the smallest module is evaluated again and again, every time with slightly different parameters. With programs, nothing happens if they are not read by a CPU incessantly, never missing a beat.

This is obviously the polar opposite of how rarely details of legal prose are looked at – usually only after something else went wrong and it all went to court, i.e. only as an exception – and it created a different culture and required a different set of tools for creation, handling and testing. With contracts becoming programs those tools can now be borrowed from IT to establish the correctness of modularized contracts. This will increase productivity and quality and organically nudge towards less ambiguity as more details can be spelled out *and kept in sync* across a larger contract at much lower cost.

In the long run, because Lexon will allow way higher complexity of rules while at the same time making them more transparent and their application guaranteed fair, it may help to integrate disenfranchised parts of society under the umbrella of one unified jurisdiction. This is worth noting because the call to preserve ambiguity can be code for a wish to leave open the space that is required for informal but very real rules to exist.

Contracts constitute private law, and to the extent that sections of a society, rich as well as poor, regard the law as geared against them and maybe even as their true social responsibility to subvert it, Lexon does not require a change of heart to get started. It will not be used to increase the reach of the law of the official jurisdiction first but can be employed to express informal parallel rules that have emerged with no enforcement through the legal system available. A blockchain's capacity to obsolete courts will effectively reduce frictions with the legal system that can arise from illegal enforcement. While in the very long run an entire legal system might migrate to a language like Lexon and in the process in fact get harder to ignore, on the way, a common ground of fairness, predictability and universal access to justice may be discovered, based on the improvements blockchains can bring and that allows where possible to integrate into the official jurisdiction the chosen rules of parts of society that before could not because the complexity this would have entailed would have been unmanageable. Where values clash, this road will be longer. But where the reality today is that cost of access to justice cuts parts of society out, and a reaction to this is reality, Lexon *is* the cure of the cause, and at the same time a possible path to establish a roof that has room for both the established official and unofficial rule sets to be joined to a consistent whole.

The Limits of Deduction

Aristotle's syllogisms that shaped Western thought, are all about finding eternal truth by way of *deduction*. That's what *συλλογισμός* means and its nature is to apply the universal to the specific. This is congruent to a top-down approach like the project *Legalese*[49] that would attempt to codify the Constitution and hope to, once done, get more specific from there.

Lexon, however, had as a rigid guiding principle to keep the focus on the low-level, actually working blockchain smart contracts first, and maybe work its way up, leaving undetermined the maximal elevation this approach could yield. [50] Which is *inductive* in spirit, going from the particular to the universal, precisely the perspective that modernity amended Aristoteles' logic with since the 19th century. Our natural sciences all rest on the pragmatic assumption that an experiment will yield the same result when repeated faithfully, even though that is strictly speaking not proving anything.[51] This is our definition of what is *scientific*. This is not an attempt to deny climate change but can we be clear that this is not deductive and therefore, will not yield 'truth.' It yields scientific predictions: useful but not strictly speaking 'knowledge.' This is relevant because logic got stuck on the puristic but impractical side for millennia, which lead to the legal profession divorcing it in anger.

Programming, like practicing law, is 'by nature' deductive: arguing in eternal hard truths.[52] But programs that interact

---

[49] Wong Meng Weng is the man. His treasure trove – https://legalese.com

[50] The founders of Legalese and Lexon hope to meet in the middle.

[51] A turkey may form opinions about the perfectly dependable law of nature that makes food appear every morning until it doesn't. This is why scientists talk about *models* that help to predict what will happen even though they might not *explain* anything, and cannot be expected to be fully reliable.

[52] *"Perhaps 90 percent of legal issues can be resolved by deduction"* – Aldisert, Clowney, Peterson, 2007: How to Think Like a Lawyer – http://ssrn.com/abstract=966597

with human beings in a dialog are of course acting on an incomplete dataset until the last input is done. This is like a contract over the course of its lifetime: the final result is for a while not clear. Both are in a certain 'state' at any given time, that changes when something relevant happens. Eventually, both programs and contracts might terminate and divulge a result. But they can wait for the next input for an extended amount of time. Many programs are not in the world to deliver one result in the end but to provide an on-going service. There are a hundred programs that are currently waiting for your next input on your phone, laptop, TV, car or watch. Often these programs have no concrete end-point but continue until shut off (or not).

This is different from how programs and computers were first imagined. But the stop-and-go is an essential element of how both contracts and smart contracts on the blockchain function. This is far removed from a deductive end-run, starting from a perfect and true dataset to the one and only valid result. Because their information is incomplete at all times, many programs are constantly creating and discarding again models about the world around them, make predictions on a best effort-basis, labor diligently to flush decayed data out of their system, and generalize from the limited subset of facts they know to conclude what their environment at large – in 'truth' – might actually look like. This is *inductive* reasoning, the way our brains actually work when we don't do math. Well, even when we do math.

Law being a practical business, embracing the messiness of life, lies and faulty memory – logical induction, based on evidence and likeliness instead of elusive 'facts' looks like an excellent fit. Inductive reasoning is unappealing in so far as it allows only to talk about *probabilities*, never of truth. But what it has going for it is, that it works, the whole of today's science is proof for that. And what forever disqualifies deductive logic is that the closed-world universe that it would work in does not actually exist. Both programming and law have gone through this revelation.

The Evolution of Logic

> *"In any state whatsoever, a judicial matter is better treated, the less is left to the decision of the judge (Plato, Laws, Book ix; Aristotle, Rhetoric, Book i; Menochius, De Arbitrariis Judicum, Book i)"[53]*

> Gottfried Leibniz, 1666

A Ph.D. of law, Leibniz, is regarded as the 'first computer scientist,' a contemporary of the 17th century no less. He proposed a Glass Bead Game in *De Arte Combinatoria* in 1666, which has been called the theoretical ancestor of modern computers.[54] The first example he gives for its application, is a legal question: the automation of the determination who a contract favors, enumerating the combinations that could result from Gaius, Digest XVII, 17.1.2:[55]

The obligation of mandate is contracted between us
whether I entrust you
only with my business,
or whether I charge you only with that of another party,
or with his along with mine,
or with my business and yours
or with yours and that of another.
Where I direct you to attend to a matter which
concerns you alone, the mandate is superfluous, and
no obligation whatever arises from it.

Fig 13 – The first ever program proposal

---

[53] De Arte Combinatoria, transl. by Loemker – https://www.math.ucla.edu/~pak/hidden/papers/Quotes/Leibniz-Arte-Combinatoria.pdf

[54] https://www.britannica.com/topic/De-Arte-Combinatoria

[55] translated by S. P. Scott. – https://www.constitution.org/sps/sps04.htm. The original: http://www.thelatinlibrary.com/justinian/digest17.shtml

This is where programming started.[56] Leibniz also immediately remarked upon a bug: 'mine, yours and that of another' is missing as 7th case. What Leibniz was hoping for, was a way to automate the decision in a concrete case, according to this law.

In the same text he also proposes that this *art* would help forming cases, likening the legal craft to geometry:

> *"The elements are simples; in geometry figures,*
> *a triangle, a circle etc.; in jurisprudence an action, a*
> *promise, a sale etc. Cases are combinations of these,*
> *which are infinitely variable in either field."*[57]

This reflects Leibniz' view that everything should be expressible as a com2nation[58] of basic concepts.

To be clear, this is the paper that is called the beginning of computer sciences. It was written by a Ph.D. of law and the first proposal for a program ever written was to program an ancient law. The intuition then that programming and law have a similar nature predates the advent of computers. In fact, law was one of the major inspirations to start thinking about programs at all. In that sense, if we succeed to join programming and law it will really be programming coming full circle, finally arriving what it had first been imagined for. If we find that it is a surprisingly powerful fit, it may actually not be surprising at all, because programming was conceived this way in the first place: to work for law. It was just forgotten on the way.

Leibniz did not only do law and the *Ars Combinatoria* also includes examples for philosophy and mathematics. He was a polymath and turned his attention to whatever suited. But his official post was that of Privy Counselor of Justice, one of his two formal educations was in law and he was a practicing

---

[56] This is not a program; it is the idea for a program. The first program was written by Charles Babbage in 1836, or Ada Lovelace, in 1842. For her 'Notes,' see: http://www.fourmilab.ch/babbage/sketch.html#NoteG

[57] Arte, Ibid.

[58] That's really how he spelled it. He was the first script kiddie, too.

lawmaker, involved in a sizeable law reform. His work is not just a footnote to computer sciences but regarded as foundational contribution. In a dream-like sequence he all but predicted the punch card, which was central to the separation of program and machine – in a vision of marbles falling through holes.[59]

Throughout his life, Leibniz thought and wrote about a universal formal language he called *characteristica universalis* that would allow for unambiguous reasoning – N.B. not just number crunching. [60] He also built some of the earliest mechanical calculators.[61] But he understood the difference between language and formula,[62] possibly even between program and hardware.[63] He knew that he needed a *language* first to be able

---

[59] *"This calculus could be implemented by a machine (without wheels), in the following manner, easily to be sure and without effort. A container shall be provided with holes in such a way that they can be opened and closed. They are to be open at those places that correspond to a 1 and remain closed at those that correspond to a 0. Through the opened gates small cubes or marbles are to fall into tracks, through the others nothing. It is to be shifted from column to column as required."* – Leibniz 1679, *De Progressione Dyadica.* published in E. Hochstetter, H.-J. Greve, eds., 1995: *Herrn von Leibniz' Rechnung mit Null und Einz*; translated by V. Huber-Dyson; quoted after: https://www.edge.org/discourse/schirrmacher_eurotech.html.

George Dyson comments: *"In the shift registers at the heart of all electronic computers, from mainframes to microprocessors, voltage gradients and pulses of electrons have taken the place of gravity and marbles, but otherwise things are still running exactly as Leibniz envisioned."*

[60] *"It is true that in the past I planned a new way of calculating suitable for matters which have nothing in common with mathematics, and if this kind of logic were put into practice, every reasoning, even probabilistic ones, would be like that of the mathematician: if need be, the lesser minds which had application and good will could, if not accompany the greatest minds, then at least follow them. For one could always say: let us calculate, and judge correctly through this, as much as the data and reason can provide us with the means for it. But […] it seems that mankind is still not mature enough to lay claim to the advantages which this method could provide."* – Leibniz, 1706. Letter to Electress Sophia.

[61] The principle of the Leibniz Wheel being in use until the 1970s – https://en.wikipedia.org/wiki/Leibniz_wheel

[62] He invented the notation for calculus that is still in use today.

[63] Experts can't fully agree if the *calculus ratiocinator* he proposed was software or hardware.

to write the formulas that could make a machine reason about more than numbers.

Leibniz' fascination with Chinese culture led him to believe that atoms of meaning should be expressible in individual symbols. Descartes had proposed that such a universal language should be based on a very limited number of primitives. Leibniz established the notion that a separate layer of meaning existed behind language that could be used to automate reasoning if a better way to express it could be found. This leads directly to one of the main controversies of 20th century linguistics (pg. 354).

The mathematician Frege later referred to Leibniz' vision in his work on a *"formula language, modeled on pure thought"* (*Begriffsschrift*, 1879), which was a foundation of first-order logic, the first major step beyond Aristotle. Frege's idiosyncratic, two-dimensional notation[64] was in turn used by Zuse to create the first higher programming language, Plankalkül, in 1942. This makes for only two hops and one mathematician between the vision of the lawmaker and an electrical engineer for the invention of higher programming languages. [65] But it took 250 years.

Frege's notation for logical reasoning replaced *subject* and *predicate* by *argument* and *function*. A concept that Loglan (pg. 354) implements – with limited success – for a human language that should enable clearer thought. Lexon dials this back for all cases when *natural* grammar is dealt with. But technically keeps part of Frege's formalism in how it bundles bits of meaning into *clauses*. In this way Lexon's syntax differentiates between, on the one hand, a-priori patterns (of the language itself) that Lexon re-aligns with natural language grammar as found in syllogisms – versus, on the other hand, the subject matter of a text (the intention of a contract, listed in clauses)

---

[64] Types annotated in a separate row.

[65] The analogous US/British pantheon might be Newton, Peirce, Backus.

that in Lexon is modeled on how functions work in modern program languages. In a way Lexon comes back to law after the science of logic has matured to a self-assured stage, ready to dress up as natural language again, a form it had shed 140 years ago to find clarity first. But the concept of a 'function' had meanwhile evolved during its time in practical programming and plays a different, essential role now in extending the 'vocabulary' of a document. Lexon thus uses the old style (speech) for the basics that all contracts share, the new style (clauses) to add logic specific to the contract. Which is very much how both contracts and programs are crafted. Lexon just unifies the looks.

The symbolic logic one learns in school today may appear as timeless as Euclide's geometry but is in fact very young. It originates from Boole's *The Mathematical Analysis of Logic*, the first rigidly structured approach to logic, developed as recently as 1847. Its current looks were contributed by Paeno in 1888. The symbol ∧ for 'and' is only from 1930: right before programming became a thing. It is this logic that Lexon proposes over Deontic logic, a basis that virtually all programming languages share (pg. 114).

Logic has only recently – in 1931 – become self-aware and come to understand its own hard limits, literally by Gödel proving logically that no logical system can prove itself. It sounds like an ordinary hen-egg insight but the point is that the hen got it and it was a big shock that impacted the mathematical community. It brought one of their dearest projects to a shuttering halt, right before the dawn of computing in the 1940s. To prove his point, Gödel had to reach outside of mathematics in a way, to reason about it from the outside. Mathematically. He invented a kind of meta-math, assigning numbers to formulas and proofs, to represent them in his proof. In the formula to prove things about formulas and proofs. At this point, math became programming: while finding a way to express a self-reflecting insight about math, in math. This power of abstraction, the capability to reach beyond itself, is what programming started with.

The point here is that for Computational Law to happen, not only had the hardware been missing the last millennia but crucially the math. This is relevant because Computational Law is not dead set on being computed by a computer. The focus is on the method, which could on a smaller scale be executed by human assistants. Which in theory means the Romans could have done it, or anyone else in the 2,000 years since. Except they could not because programming had yet to be invented.

The Reality of Programming

When programming finally arrived, it was at first in the form of extremely primitive command lists that would be fed a mechanical central processing unit to execute hardwired sub tasks like addition or subtraction. These lists were necessarily technical step-by-step *instructions* rather than logical formulas.

A program could be the instruction to 'load' a certain number – say, 3 – into a 'register' – a special place in the machine, maybe called *A-register* –, then another number – say, 5 – into another register – *B* – and finally execute the 'add' command. Register *A* would then hold the result, 8. 'Load into A' may have been assigned the command number 1 (binary 00001), 'load into B', 2, 'add A and B', number 3. The code might thus have been 1 3, 2 5, 3:

```
00001 00011
00010 00101
00011
```

Fig 14 – Binary program code example

Years later, imperative code like this would say the same thing:

```
A = 3
B = 5
A = A + B
```

Fig 15 – Structured program code example

Backus, the inventor of BNF (pg. 144), criticized that the re-definition of A (in the example in line 3) was breaking the algebraic mold. Programming as it emerged, shaped by the primitive machines that were the first computers, somehow was getting the notion of variables wrong. Command lists like this were not really math. In math, A, once defined, cannot suddenly become something else. The usefulness of a mathematical formula entirely rests on this. That programming had turned out like this was because of the limited number of staging grounds, the registers, that a central processing unit could handle. Variables were re-used as a matter of prudence. It took many decades for programming languages to come around to how math does it; the mainstream languages of today still haven't.

And already in 1936 Turing had proven that not every program was going to be computable, not even if the dataset and the algorithm were fully known. His proof was based on Gödel's and included – only then – the first mathematical definition of a computer program. His find was as disappointing as Gödel's. The 'Halting Problem' is one reason for why Ethereum needs to count gas every step of the way: it cannot be determined a-priori how many steps certain programs will need to make, or if they will ever finish at all. In Ethereum, there is a check every step, if the gas has run out, not least to prevent unpredictable dead loops[66] that would crash the entire chain. This is very pricy though and many normal programs don't have

---

[66] A dead loop is a program error where a loop can never be exited. For example, the code **a = 1; while (a > 0) do a = a + 1;** is practically a dead loop. Turing essentially proved that one cannot prove that a program has no such never-ending behavior.

this check, which is the reason why computers 'crash,' or 'hang:' they get lost in a dead loop with no way to recognize the problem and get out of it. They can ultimately not fully reflect their own actions. Programs today are many magnitudes more complex than what Turing reasoned about but the principle holds.

Nasty 'bugs' kept programmers busy from the start. A program should run but it did not. Or, worse, it ran mostly but sometimes not. What Turing had shown also meant that there would be hard limits to how much computers themselves would be able to help to get programs right. The actual work of programmers included probing, testing and puzzling. It was not the exact science that could have been expected on the premise that programs are essentially formulas reasoning about perfectly logical deductions. The reality of programming had become a step-by-step process in every way, intuitive as mathematics always were, a craft where experience mattered, and a sharp mind and painstaking diligence, but formal logic reasoning only rarely. Might sound familiar to jurists.

Only in 1972 did a language emerge – Prolog – that implemented the discovery that the *imperative* (step-by-step) listing of a program and its *declarative*, logical notation could be expressed as one. This was at the end of a long flame war in the AI community over whether it made any sense to represent knowledge in imperative style at all, or if it had to be in a declarative way – looking more like math and predicate logic – to be of any help for AI. Prolog's syntax manages to do both at the same time. It looks somewhat like a syllogism but doubles as an instruction list that can be executed top-down:

```
grandmother(X, Y) :-
    mother(X, Z),
    mother(Z, Y).
```

Fig 16 – Prolog code example

On the one hand this expresses the 'static' declaration that

X is the grandmother of Y, in case (i.a.) that
X is the mother of Z and Z is the mother of Y.

But it can also be 'executed' as a step-by-step instruction list:

To test whether X might be the grandmother of Y:
test if X is the mother of Z and Z the mother of Y.

This is the starting point for Lexon. Obviously, Prolog remained with Frege's substitution of subject-and-predicate prose by a function-and-argument notation. To say, Prolog does *not* read:

> X is the grandmother of Y, if ...

However, this is a matter of syntax rather than substance. Both forms could result into the same AST (pg. 123).

Lexon is not just Prolog with some natural language sugar coating. But the initial hypothesis was based on experimentation with a similarly basic building block. Instead of Prolog's lingering between declarative and imperative notation, Lexon's grammar spans both natural and computer language. The central question in both cases was the same: how far can we go so that a machine can still unambiguously read this.

Higher-Order Logic

Today's computer programs are *higher-order logic*. The step that goes beyond *first-order logic* is that they can reason logically about themselves to some degree, for example about the types of their variables (is x a number or a list of numbers?) or treat their own code as data (x can be a function). Code creates code for the most mundane tasks now: most big webpages consist of code created by other code on the fly, optimized by yet other code, over multiple levels. What did not really happen are programs that would write themselves, which is different. The systems that automatically produce the code for webpages are themselves laboriously coded by humans. The delineation up to where humans work and from where computers take over is often very clear because it is the front line where the debugging happens. We did not yet manage to teach computers to code.[67]

However, for Leibniz, where we got would be so utterly mind-boggling!

The Boolean Truth
of Efficient Breach

Meanwhile in law, the theory of Efficient Breach appeared that posits:

> *"Repudiation of obligations should be encouraged where the promisor is able to profit from his default after placing his promisee in as good a position as he would have occupied had performance been rendered."*[68]

In other words, if a party to a contract feels they would be better off by breaking the contract, even after paying to make the other party hole, then this should be welcomed as the best option for aggregate welfare of society, and not punished in court. The proposal was made as an attempt to explain why

---

[67] This looks like the great failure of the 5th generation of computer languages. They were supposed to disintermediate the programmers. There were massive efforts in the 80s to achieve this that faltered in the 90s.

[68] Robert Birmingham, 1970: "Breach of Contract, Damage Measures, and Economic Efficiency"; 24 Rutgers L. Rev. 273.

common law developed such that it did rarely force a party in breach to perform as promised, and also usually not levied punishment on top of expectation damages, but mostly just ordered the promisor in breach to pay for the promisee's lost profits. The theory only made official what had already become the practice. But it does do away with all pretense that the Deontic terminology of a contract should be interpreted to carry any moral meaning. Which it could because breaching the promise of a contract had already stopped coming at stifling reputational cost.

This makes the language of "shall" and "must" in contracts out of date. If everything in a contract is optional, if at a cost, this makes blockchain smart contracts and their Boolean Logic of "true" and "false" the more appropriate framework to articulate contracts in.

Because blockchains were developed with commercial transactions in mind, it is fair to speculate that they might have turned out differently if contracts still had a moral, i.e. reputational dimension. But as it stands, reputation systems have become a much-debated staple of blockchain discussions but they are not built into the deeper fabric.

One can argue that Efficient Breach only works for commodified product chains where it is sufficiently predictable what the lost profit would have been. The power balance between the parties has to be roughly equal so one can't just outspend the other in court. The contract must be big enough that going to court is a risk worth taking in the first place.[69] This will hit the small players,[70] the innovative, unpredictable business.

---

[69] Note that the brocard *pacta sunt servanda* as well as the *principle of good faith*, which are foundational tenets of civil law as well as international law, do not exist in common law jurisdictions.

[70] "American markets, ... are giving up on healthy competition. Sector after economic sector is more concentrated than it was twenty years ago, dominated by fewer and bigger players who lobby politicians aggressively to protect and expand their profit margins. Across the country, this drives up

It may maximize the economic outcome for society on average and in the moment, at the detriment of the weaker party to a contract, as well as of progress at large as commodification occurs as a rule only after a domain matures. If one looks at cars, rocket ships, super-sonic planes or affordability of housing, there is an argument possible that this might be happening since the 70s. Maybe the argument that the breach of a contract can be the moral thing to do, argued by a judge less, is a sign of the times.

Blockchain smart contracts however make the modern take on what a contract is visible and allow to express it in a straight forward way: the cost of breach is spelled out, in arbitrary detail and variation. The fees for it might be staked – i.e. paid in up front so that the punishment can be executed automatically. The non-breaching party then does not have to go to court and both sides have clarity going in what exactly a breach will cost and that it will be paid.

Importantly, when articulated in this way, a digital contract is not even 'broken' when an Efficient Breach is elected. It just leaves its 'happy path.'[71] All of the procedure of handling the 'breach' is part of the contract, it has become one of the available options. It can be programmed so that at that point everything is handed over to a human arbiter or court. Or it can be fully automated, needing no outside intervention, triggered by one of the parties, or a missed deadline. The automation is a spectrum. While the natural way to write contracts for a blockchain will be to make everything an option and thus spell out all possible Efficient Breach conditions and include them into the explicit contract – one can also implement the opposite, using the court system as fallback.

---

prices while driving down investment, productivity, growth, and wages, resulting in more inequality." – T. Philippon, The Great Reversal, 2019

[71] In programming, the *happy path* is the core intended functionality. It can be a minuscule part of the whole, which adds error and other exception handling and generally takes care of all alternate, if less frequent cases.

But to the extent that options, including to breach, are included in the text of a digital contract, the procedures described for them *cannot be broken*. There is no breach of the breach procedures possible. If it is all automated and staked, there is no way to refuse to pay for the lost profits or ignore a deadline. The unbreakable nature of blockchain smart contracts creates a powerful, fast and cost efficient, unstoppable mechanism right below the layer where everything is optional.

Digital contracts thus protect the smaller players from the risk and cost of litigation, especially in the case of Efficient Breach. This should make market participation viable for a broader spectrum of participants and safeguard innovation against the power and deep pockets of incumbents.

Sufficient Probability as Facts

Lexon approached Computational Law with the same resolve to *accept incompleteness* that fuels the aversion of many lawyers against the call for a less ambiguous method for contracting. Accepting the limits of the knowable is the right reason why legal professionals make a point that their business cannot be that of justice. The same reason instructs scientists to speak only of *predictions* and *confidence-levels*, instead of truth.

But fascinatingly, moving away from hard facts is also at the heart of how blockchains solved the seemingly intractable problem of a copy protection for digital data. Which is the basis for how blockchains can furnish digital cash without a central bank: it had been 'known' that no two computers could reliably agree on a fact *and also know* that they agree.[72] This remains

---

[72] This is called *The Two General's Problem* –
https://en.wikipedia.org/wiki/Two_Generals%27_Problem

true. What Bitcoin introduced with *proof-of-work*[73] – for all its flaws – was a switch from 'knowing facts' to make the best of *sufficient probability*.

That all of our science is based on observation instead of truth has led to heated discussions among philosophers about the nature of inductive reasoning as recently as the mid 20th century.[74] It is only prudent that the legal domain stayed out of that crossfire. What is not disputed is that induction works. The way that blockchains use it is dumbfounding for programmers because it essentially replaces facts with best-guesses and overwhelming likeliness. It feels wrong and sloppy at first – but it works. O deal in probabilities instead of truth, sure reminds of quantum physics. And it really provided for a quantum leap.

Through this shift, blockchain technology creates a shared world view – an artificial truth shared across many computers – that had been thought to be impossible.[75] This shared view – the *consensus* – is material for a blockchains to work and enables many other applications beyond crypto currencies. But because of how this consensus is achieved,[76] 'knowledge' of each participant about 'the truth' is never absolute but only very, very likely. Which for practical reasons is sufficient the same way that we find it reasonable to assume that the sun will come up tomorrow (by induction), although there is no way to

---

[73] *Proof-of-work* is the mechanism that Bitcoin uses to find a useable illusion of consensus between the computers participating in its network.

[74] Wikipedia can't even decide whether a quote from Prof. Gillies should stand that claims that rules of inductive reasoning exist in AI. – https://en.wikipedia.org/w/index.php?title=Inductive_reason-ing&oldid=934496424. Footnote 35 holds the claim but in apt self-similarity is annotated as "failed verification" where it is used in the main text..

[75] The Two General's Problem describes the impossibility to be certain that an appointment is made and also confirmed as messengers might get lost.

[76] There are different consensus mechanisms and some methods, like .e.g. 'proof-of-stake' have a firmer guarantee for the shared truth. They most of the time have disadvantages, e.g. with less scale usually, being unable to include thousands of computers as Bitcoin, Ethereum or Aeternity do.

prove it (by deduction). Past observations are convincing enough that world commerce rests on the assumption that there is a tomorrow.

Jurists are completely right when they insist that it makes no sense to talk in absolutes: the blockchain cannot, either. But just like law and science, it has embraced probability as workable model and it is within this framework that the Boolean *true* and *false* values of smart contracts exist. It is not real truth, it can suffer catastrophic technical failure.[77] But that is true of anything on this planet. For most intents and purposes, it simply works and in connection with money transfers it is qualitatively a new reality – one where **true** and **false** are so reliably accessible – infinitesimally less than 100% – that it does make sense to allow reasoning based on such comfortable black-and-white terms.

This should be complemented with the Efficient Breach, the realistic view of contractual obligations as options that are fulfilled precisely when it makes economic sense. It then becomes inevitable that contracts should more and more be expressed in *true* and *false*, instead of permissions, obligations and prohibitions. The kind of ambiguity that this eliminates, will not be missed. And because of the limitations of Deontic Logic, the benefit is automated reasoning, in a transparent way: the ability to perform 'mechanized' legal analysis.

Legal professionals should leave the instinctive reaction to distrust absolutes behind and not reject calls for less ambiguity out of hand, the same way that programmers embraced probability. We could meet in the middle, on new ground.

---

[77] But Lexon was made to protect the technology against weaponized law when the technology works right (pg. 117). Not to block remedy through the court of law if the technology fails. Lexon really expresses intent. If the automation fails, because the blockchain underneath does, the code will still express what should have happened. And this case is altogether less likely though than a frivolous suit attacking a smart contract claiming that it did not perform as announced.

The Power of Types

Does Lexon realize Leibniz' dream? Well, Leibniz would probably have been happy with FORTRAN.[78] As a polymath he would have been the lawyer who learned coding to be able to automate reasoning. No need of Lexon in that sense. The chore-oriented way that he meant it, computers can do since long. Lexon adds inclusion of everyone else, and the interface, through natural language, to our legal system as it exists today.

And as a good riddle, Leibniz' quest might have been a bit of a trick question. Leibniz' *characteristica universalis* are interpreted as the idea of a *universal language* and the main quest for it to be for its base vocabulary. The characteristics were to be combined but always in the same, generic fashion. Presumably, absolute concepts should have been found, like what Llull hat proposed 400 years earlier: *goodness, greatness, eternity, power, wisdom, will, virtue, truth,* and *glory.* But Leibniz did not commit, to the extent that Gödel, who collected all about it, started to suspect that parts of Leibniz' writing about the *characteristica* was missing and actively suppressed.

However, disappointingly prosaically, the 'universal characteristics' are probably really *types*, i.e. 'person', 'amount' or 'time'. 'Characteristics' isn't a bad label for types. Types signify the absolute that is known about a name, e.g. that the "Buyer" is a *person*, before the actual person or number or point in time is known. That is, all that is known about a name when writing a template, which is not a concrete contract yet. The type is the only thing understood about the names, because the computer does *not* understand the meaning of the word 'buyer.' From the line '**"Buyer" is a person**' it does understand that it is a

---

[78] The first higher programming language in commercial use, conceived by Backus in 1953, more on the math side of things, and to this day a standard in high-performance computing. The author's father described his excitement waiting for a FORTRAN compiler to become available on his university's machine. Those were the quantum leaps.

person. But it has no concept of what a 'buyer' is, it is but a label for humans. It actually gets stripped out and replaced by a number when the code is compiled for the machine.

Types are also what makes programming higher-order logic and how different programming languages use different types in differently ways, is a major differentiator among them. It's one of the most important categories whether a language is hard-, soft-, statically or dynamically typed (Lexon is statically hard-typed).

Types also determine what verbs a name can be used with. Only persons can certify. Only amounts can be paid. As it turns out, the 'reasoning' that Leibniz looked for really rests on the meta-data that is expressed in these relationships between names. The cobweb that verbs extend between names *is* the actual meaning of the contract. One can copy-paste a contract many times, if only the names of persons, times and amounts are changed, the logic of all these agreements remains the same. What defines the logic of a contract are the individual relationships in it. They are actually the more useful expression, e.g. of what a 'buyer' is in the *concrete* context of a concrete contract – more useful than what the pseudo-universal, but really blurry meaning of the word 'buyer' could offer (pg. 150).

At any rate, types *are* probably the magic portal through which all of law, including the less procedural statutes could be made computable. The break through might be achieved by dropping the quest to find a way to express the less procedural statutes as *executable code* – what Lexon can do today – but to adopt instead a perspective **of the more general provisions as type declarations** that can by nature be dynamic, also anonymous, i.e. definitions that have no explicit name to them. The act of interpretation of law – matching a case to a statute – would be *late binding* or dynamic *duck typing*: a process of rule-finding by *forward chaining interference* as e.g. known from the production system OPS5.[79] The dataset being the contract and its state; and the rules, obviously, the statutes or precedence.

As is often the case with the application of blockchain, the work of the attorneys to find precedence or statute that convincingly matches a concrete case, is *shifted forward*, taken out of the hands of attorneys and laid into the hands of lawyers instead who at the time of the creation of a contract would make explicit what 'framework' i.e. what statutes a contract to be written should be plugged into. Seen from the programming side this would resemble the decision what *modules* to *include* and what *framework objects* or what *actor behavior* to *inherit* from: the process of assigning type to tap into the operations available for it. This would mean that the crafting of a contract anchors it in the choice of law that should govern it – which of course will be possible only once **digital law** expressed in Lexon exists in the first place. The point here is whether and how it could ever work.

Type systems are ubiquitous in software development and their major role is to be reduce errors.[80] Contracts will benefit in the same way from the use of types, i.e. from plugging into digital law: it will be provable a-priori that the contract is both legally correct and that the choice of law or precedent that it is proposed to stand on will be correct.

This may be hard to imagine now but this principle is at the heart of the more elaborate programming languages today that seek to spot as many problems in a program before it is even started by utilizing strong type systems. Many early and simpler programming languages do not have type systems though and that is (almost) where we are starting with Lexon.

---

[79] Charles Forgy: OPS5 – http://www.pcai.com/web/ai_info/pcai_ops.html

[80] E.g. the type system of *Haskell* – a favorite of mathematicians – is like a program language on its own. The new language *Rust* has as its major distinction a grueling new type system that is awful to use and to look at but makes Rust programs marvelously fast, versatile and most of all, robust.

PROCESSING MEANING

"[Regulation] requiring companies to explain decisions reached by artificial intelligence (AI) seemingly failed to grasp just how complex machine learning was becoming."[81]

Financial Times

This section explains how Lexon is different from other computer languages. It has a technical subject matter but does not require prerequisite technical knowledge. This context has helped others to get a better idea of Lexon's potential and understand how to write digital contracts.

---

[81] Daniel Winter: Too much information? The new challenge for decision-makers; Financial Times 12/13/19.

Abstract Syntax Trees

At the heart of Lexon's power lies the *Abstract Syntax Tree* (AST), an intermediate format that every compiler[82] is translating its input (program code) to, so as to then create its output (executable programs) from. So does Lexon.

To quote Wikipedia, an AST is:

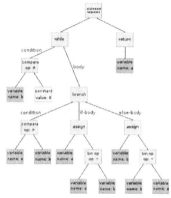

Fig 17 – AST example from Wikipedia

> *"a tree representation of the abstract syntactic structure of source code written in a programming language … 'abstract' in the sense that it does not represent every detail appearing in the real syntax, but rather just the structural, content-related details."* [83]

The tree reflects the program that it was created from, which will usually be speaking of things like *files*, *data* and *algorithms*. The novelty is that Lexon creates an AST *directly from the legal prose* of a contract, resulting into an AST that consists of *subjects*, *objects* and *predicates*, which in its very structure captures the structure of a document and of natural language, and

---

[82] A compiler – by and large – is a program that reads program code that a programmer has written to create a new program, and turns it into machine code that a computer can execute, thereby bringing to new program into existence.

[83] https://en.wikipedia.org/wiki/Abstract_syntax_tree

therefore captures more high-level 'meaning' than ASTs of other languages.

It is because the Lexon language is closer to human language, that the resulting AST shapes up closer to human thought and natural language grammar. This allows for output that is likewise closer to how humans communicate. Because with Lexon, *relationships between entities* are stored in the way that humans reason about them. And as is well known today, this metadata – the relationships – can be very powerful.

Lexon crosses a crucial threshold by being *fully* conformant to natural language grammar. This results into a quantum leap of sorts that does not happen as long as a language just edges close. It does not matter in this regard that Lexon's readability is achieved by defining a *subset* of natural language grammar, instead of being able to handle just any prose.

Beyond the grammar, the *document structure* also plays a key role for Lexon's readability. It is also reflected in a Lexon AST (Fig 28, pg. 138).

Everything else follows from there. The parsing and compilation process to create an AST is per se not special, every compiler does this. But because of its higher abstraction level, the Lexon AST captures something that ASTs normally do not: the abstract 'meaning' of a text.

A Thought Experiment

The difference in abstraction levels can be illustrated by contrasting Lexon to the program language of choice for Ethereum, Solidity.[84] A frequent question is if one could also (automatedly) translate from Solidity to Lexon – i.e. the other

---

[84] Solidity is the most popular program language for blockchain smart contracts. It is the main language of Ethereum, i.e. to create code running on the Ethereum blockchain or on any private or enterprise clone of it. See Fig 4 on pg. 18 for how it looks.

way around than what Lexon is made for. This is an understandable request, as many projects have invested in Solidity programs and now realize that it would be nice to have them as readable as Lexon code.

The question is interesting in many ways. However, the *incorrect but truthful* answer to it is "No:" translation from Solidity to Lexon is not possible in the sense that people mean it. This is true, even though '*technically*' it would have to be a "Yes:" it *is* certainly possible to automatedly translate Solidity into Lexon, because both are Turing Complete languages.[85]

But the answer is "No" regarding the *intent* of people's question, which is: would it be possible to get nicely *readable* Lexon code from such inverse translation. That would not quite be the case.

The result would be more readable than the Solidity code, offering the same 0-learning curve regarding both *grammar* and *vocabulary*. But it would show the lower-level structure of Solidity, not that of the human thought behind it, not the 'business logic'. Smart contracts of realistic complexity would turn out logically convoluted – reflective of the Solidity code – and would lack the essential feature of Lexon code: being not only written in natural language words but also structured in a coherent way, e.g. such that it can pass as the prose of a legally enforceable contract. Code translated from Solidity would not – as original Lexon code does – express in clear terms the *meeting of the minds* that a judge will be looking for, and without

---

[85] It is technically guaranteed that any program, programmed in any language, can be translated into any other language, as long as both languages are 'Turing Complete': which basically requires that both languages have variables, loops and branches. This is not a completely moot point, as for example Bitcoin and BigchainDB use transaction logic that is not Turing Complete; and the reason for the complex gas metering system in Ethereum – which counts and bills every single instruction executed – is to address a challenge that arises from allowing loops in Ethereum smart contracts.

which there may not be a legally binding agreement in the first place.

So, while you *would* end up with a working Lexon program, it would be almost as unreadable for *non-programmers* as Solidity code always is.

Words and grammar would turn out clear enough, but the logic presented would still force people to think like programmers. It is precisely the 'meaning' that the Lexon AST captures that cannot automatically be added when a Solidity program is the starting point. Because the Solidity code simply lacks this higher level of abstraction. It is actually the first step of the work of a Solidity coder, to *leave it behind*.

What Use is an AST?

The abstract syntax tree (AST) is an *intermediary step*. It is created and already deleted again in sub seconds, having helped to create *lower level* code from higher level code. Often to translate a 3rd generation language like C++, Java or Solidity down into the lowest level, the 1st generation language, called *machine code*.[86]

A compiler builds up the tree, node for node, while reading ('parsing') the human-written program text that it is to translate. The purpose of this is to pre-arrange the elements of the program into a meaningful order that will help to then create the output from a consistent, holistic description of the program: the AST. The compiler then steps through the tree, traversing all its nodes, and produces the output: e.g. a string of hexadecimal numbers, that a CPU can actually process.

An AST is a data structure in a compiler, which is itself a program. ASTs are not usually visualized, there is also no standard for them, every compiler has its own way. The AST is often not even the only data tree representation of a program during its compilation. E.g. there can be a Parse Tree before and a Document Tree after that are optimized for a specific step in the input or output.

An AST is also always used for *analysis* of the code, to check the correctness of the input (the program). This happens right after the tree is complete. And that's where in Lexon's

---

[86] With language systems like Java, C#, Erlang or Solidity, the case is more complex, because a *virtual machine* (VM) is involved. This introduces an intermediary step: the compiler compiles not into machine code but into *op codes,* a very low-level input to the virtual machine to execute at a later time. The VM is itself a program that consists of machine code, the lowest level there is. This additional step does not make a difference regarding this discussion about ASTs. The AST is still in all cases the first internal representation that a compiler creates.

case it gets very interesting, because Lexon can use the tree to analyze *legal contracts*, on the level of their *intent*.

A BASIC AST Example

If a BASIC[87] compiler (itself a program, usually written in C) processes this BASIC code snippet:

```
print 1 + 2                                    BASIC
```

Fig 18 – BASIC example program: print 1 + 2

It creates as intermediary step this AST data structure:

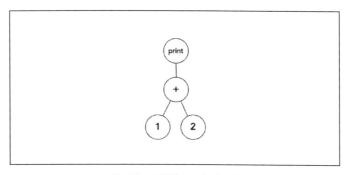

Fig 19 – AST for: print 1 + 2

From this AST snippet the compiler then creates the machine language[88] that a computer understands and can execute.

---

[87] BASIC is the most-used programming language in the world because it is built into virtually every spreadsheet software.

[88] After creating this AST from the source code, the compiler then traverses it from the top, going left where possible, down where possible, i.e. in the order: print, +, 1, 2. Whenever the traversal hits a dead end (1, 2) or comes 'back up' through a node being done with all its down-branches (+, print), results are being created. I.e. in the order: 1, 2, +, print. This is the order of things that is required by the machine language that everything has to be

Just to make a point, this will look somewhat like this:

```
10100001 10111100 10010011 00000100
00001000 00000011 00000101 11000000
10010011 00000100 00001000 10100011
```

Fig 20 – example of machine language

The tree is the intermediary step that helps the compiler to translate the BASIC code (Fig 18) to machine language (Fig 20).

But, importantly, the *same* tree would be produced by:

```
print (1 + 2)                                    BASIC
```

Fig 21 – BASIC example program: print (1+2)

Because the brackets are redundant – they don't add any meaning in this case – the compiler does away with them when determining the order of the nodes[89] of the AST.

Note that neither the programmer, nor the user of a program usually bother about the AST, nor about the machine code. We are looking at it to make a point.

---

translated to. The resulting commands in machine language will basically be: *remember 1, remember 2, add up and remember the last two things you remember, print the last thing you remember.* This is called stack-based because a useful metaphor for this way of managing values is a stack of cards on which they are put on and drawn from. Note how perfectly *anaphoric* this is as it uses no names for values, only relative, context sensitive references. An alternate way this can play out on the machine level is: *assign 1 to A, assign 2 to B, add A and B and put the result into A, print A.* This is called *register-based* and executes faster. Note that in both cases the machine needs the commands in the same order that is practically obtainable from the AST.

[89] In a tree structure, the points where branches occur, and also the end points, are called *nodes.* In this document's AST visualizations, they are the bubbles. The connections between nodes are called '*edges.*'

A Lexon AST Example

In Lexon's case, a useful code example may be:

> The "Signer" certifies the "Data."   LEXON

Fig 22 – LEXON example code: The Signer certifies the Data.

Resulting in this AST:

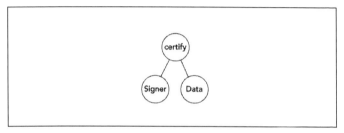

Fig 23 – AST for: "Signer" certifies "Data."

Note that – while all explained before holds – this AST clearly expresses a relationship of the natural language grammar elements *verb* (**certify**), *subject* (**Signer**), and *object* (**Data**). This is very different from the previous, more mathematical, but typical BASIC example.

But like in the BASIC example, what matters in the Lexon AST are the semantics, not the syntax: the *exact same* tree would be created by:

> "Signer" certifies "Data."   LEXON

because the missing *determiners* ("**the**") do not change the meaning. They have as little influence on the actual functionality as the missing brackets had in Fig 21.

It is also intentional that the top node of this AST snippet reads '**certify**' and not '**certifies**': the natural language inflection was discarded; this detail is not needed in the tree. In fact, the role of the inflection, to support the connection to the subject, is assumed by the *edge* that connects **Signer** and **certify** – including the fact that it is the first edge, counting from left.

ASTs focus on Meaning

As can be seen from these examples of BASIC and Lexon code, the ASTs, at heart, express the same thing as the code expresses but reduce it to the meaningful elements and store it in a way that is more suitable to the intended use: to create meaningful output from it.

A tree format has an advantage in expressiveness: while code is 1-dimensional – it only reads forward, in sequence, as any text does – a tree is multi-dimensional: each node can have many connections.[90] This is used in a tree representation to express relationships that in code have to be written sequentially – e.g. by using brackets, or by simply lining things up. As an example, a conditional branch in code may look like:

```
IF a THEN b ELSE c                          BASIC
```

Fig 24 – BASIC code example: IF a THEN b ELSE c

Logically, there is no particular reason that the ELSE part should be listed *after* the THEN part. Machine language, by the way, often has it vice versa: the else part being written before the THEN code. An AST depicts this in a clearer, two-dimensional

---

[90] In the interest of the point to be made, and for the benefit of the non-technical reader, the depiction of lists and strings in the ASTs has been simplified.

way, with one root node (**if**) and three dependent nodes (**a, b** and **c**):

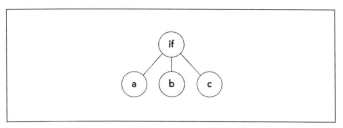

Fig 25 – AST for: if a then b else c

This paints a clearer picture of how all nodes (**a, b, c**) share the **if**-node as nexus.

Trees lack the 'sugar', as programmers call it, that makes a program more readable to the human eye, and they break out of the straight jacket of sequential order that written text has to conform to.[91] They leave out unimportant and redundant detail and normalize the logic.

ASTs abstract from Syntax

ASTs *also* do away with the idiosyncrasies of languages, some-what in passing, they just have to.

For example, the following three code examples – in the programming languages BASIC, Lisp and Lua respectively – all result in the same AST. Because they all *mean* the same, even though they look different when spelled out in three different programming languages as shown here:

---

[91] The very first higher programming language, Konrad Zuse's Plankalkül, actually used a 2-dimensional notation, following Frege's Begriffsschrift. – https://en.wikipedia.org/wiki/Plankalkül

```
LET a = 1 + 2 : PRINT a                    BASIC
```

```
(let ((a (+ 1 2))) (print a))              Lisp
```

```
a = 1 + 2; print(a)                        Lua
```

Fig 26 – same example in BASIC, Lisp and Lua.

These would all result into this abstract syntax tree:

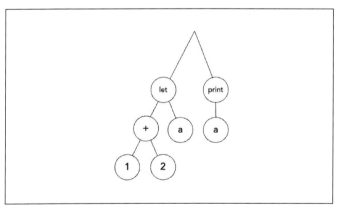

Fig 27 – multi-lingual AST for: a := 1 + 2, print a

Which illustrates how the AST is by nature something that is more abstract than a programming language: a *unifier across different languages*, focused on the payload of a program.

The AST distills the content, shedding the form it was articulated in.[92]

---

[92] Because the compilers for BASIC, Lisp and Lua are all different programs, with their own specific needs and optimizations, the respective real data

Because the languages in our example are by nature similar[93] they all produce the same abstraction, the same AST. In the inverse, this also means: these languages all *require* the same level of abstract, technical thinking from their programmers. The AST does not *add* things. Its creation is by virtue of a transformation, from a different way to write the same logic – i.e. from the source code, as written by the programmer – to the internal representation of the AST, to be able to then output what a machine can 'understand.'

Lexon, does *not* share the AST with other languages. BASIC, Lisp and Lua are languages of the 3rd and 4th generation. Lexon claims to be the first member of the 6th generation of languages.[94] Nowhere does that become clearer than how different its AST is.

---

structures used to store the ASP may be more complex. The graphic given here is a simplification but the point stands: the differences between the language syntaxes are cancelled out. Especially the order of numbers, operators and variables that is so diverse between e.g. BASIC and Lisp, is normalized to the same structure in the AST. As an aside, the AST also explains the logic behind the peculiar order of things in Lisp.

[93] BASIC and Lisp are not usually said to be similar. But they are, when compared to machine code, Assembler, or Lexon.

[94] On language generations see footnote 23, pg. 23.

ASTs and Natural Language

Lexon can convert legal prose into an AST, without loss, which in turn is made possible because the *shape of the Lexon AST reflects natural language grammar.* As is visible in the Lexon AST example in Fig 23, pg. 132: the left-hand node holds the *subject*, the right-hand node the *object* and the root node at the top, the *verb*.

Example of a Lexon AST

The Lexon AST for the escrow code from page 3, looks like this:

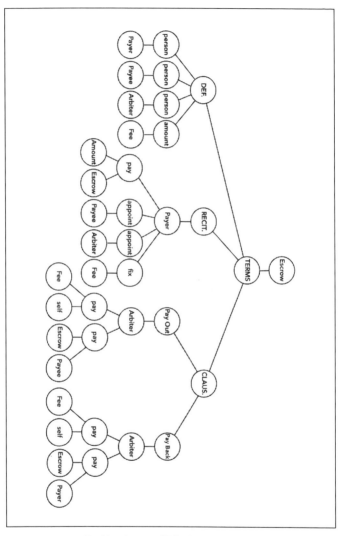

Fig 28 – Lexon AST for Escrow Example

This tree is a self-explanatory graph consisting of clause names (**Escrow, Pay Out, Pay Back**), groups (**TERMS, DEFINITIONS, RECITALS, CLAUSES**), subjects (**Payer, Arbiter**), objects

(**Amount, Escrow, Payee, Arbiter, Fee, Payer**), and verbs (**pay, appoint, fix**).

Below the nodes of the document parts (**DEFINITIONS, RECITALS, CLAUSES**) the high-level that is the document structure blends (head, definition, recital, clauses) with the grammatical level below it (subjects, verbs, objects). The AST literally shows the latter as levels below the former.

Note that all names of all *subjects* and *objects* in this AST have been freely chosen by the programmer and could be any combination of words, while the *verbs* are part of the limited base vocabulary of Lexon. This allows both for unlimited variation in crafting the contract text (through freely defined nouns) and a limit to the required learning (of verbs) to *write* Lexon code.

Example of a Solidity AST

In so far as the impression gained from the above graph may be a trivial one – "how else should it look really" – the contrast with the blockchain language of choice – Solidity – may be enlightening.

The AST given below is that of a 'native' Solidity program of similar functionality,[95] proposed by *Pranav K* on *medium*.[96] The AST is much bigger than the AST of the Lexon example, because Solidity is operating 'closer to the bits and bytes,' which is normal for a 3rd generation language like Solidity. It is therefore more verbose and needs more words to say the same thing.

---

[95] Pranav K. on medium 2017 – https://medium.com/@pranav.89/smart-contracting-simplified-escrow-in-solidity-ethereum-b19761e8fe74

[96] Fig 29 (pg. 48) serve to give an idea of the size of the AST. A more readable version of the same AST can be found in the Appendix, Fig 21, pg. 68.

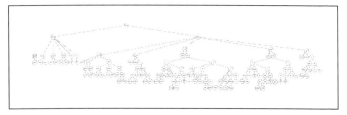

Fig 29 – Solidity AST for a Similar Escrow Example

From the labels of the nodes – see the cut out, Fig 30, below – it is apparent that this AST is concerned with a completely *different world,* a different set of elements and patterns. There are no subjects, objects and verbs but *object references, function calls* and *parameters* instead.

The cut out below shows the *payout* functionality. As can be seen, a different, more conventional concept of a program is revealed, that has nothing to do with natural language. The functionality shown in the tree can be cobbled together with a bit of study (and that can be fun), but it is not obvious, instead rather confusing as to the intended purpose – i.e. the 'meaning' of it all.

It is apparent that this Solidity AST is fundamentally different to the Lexon AST because it makes *different use of nodes*: it does not mirror natural language and its grammar instead reflects the algorithm-friendly abstractions that have become the mainstream of programming languages since the definition of ALGOL in 1958. This vernacular has become so common place that today, programmers do not really register its presence anymore. It's just how computers are programmed in this day and age. The question "how could it be any different" for *this tree,* the Solidity AST (Fig 29 & Fig 30), is as pertinent for a programmer as it is for the Lexon AST (Fig 28) for the naïve observer. It reflects how both programmers and lawyers think very differently and might find it hard to change. Lexon bridges this chasm.

For a more detailed walk through of ASTs see pg 367.

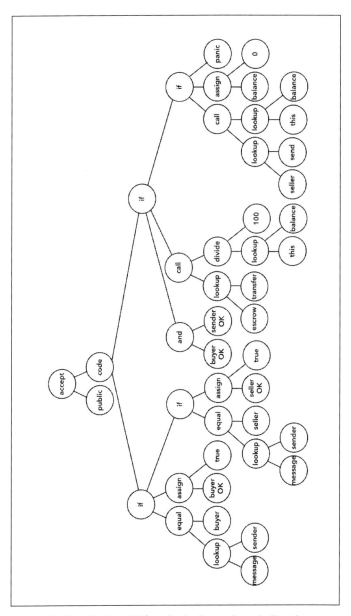

Fig 30 – Solidity AST for a Similar Escrow Example (Detail)

A More Meaningful Level of Abstraction

In the end what makes the difference is not just that Lexon's vocabulary stays closer to plain English, and not just that Lexon's grammar is 'more natural' than that of other program languages, but that Lexon's abstractions *operate on a higher level*. And this results in ASTs that express meaning that is *not present* in source code written in Solidity, and therefore also not in Solidity's ASTs. This is the essential bit that would be found missing when translating Solidity back to Lexon.

Because until now, as a required first step when programming, this high-level meaning of a program is shred to finer grained piecemeal and rendered unrecognizable. Amazingly, it is the *business logic* of a program itself that does routinely not survive impact. C. Lopes et al. in their paper *Toward Naturalistic Programming* write:

> *"Researchers are constantly looking for ways to express the programs in a form that more closely follows the way programmers think **before they are forced to break their thoughts in operational details imposed by the existing programming languages.** We know that this is possible, because when programmers are asked to explain their code, they do so concisely, skipping operational details, sometimes using a thought flow that is quite different from the control flow in the code."*[97]

The building blocks that programs are commonly created from today are just too subtle to capture the higher level. The more so, the lower-level (early-generation) the language is.

As a metaphor, the difference could be described by molecules vs. atoms: Solidity loses (or never has) the information

---

[97] C. V. Lopes, P. Dourish, D. H. Lorenz, K. Lieberherr, 2003. Beyond AOP: toward naturalistic programming. SIGPLAN Not. 38, 12 (December 2003), 34-43. DOI=http://dx.doi.org/10.1145/966051.966058 – emphasis added.

about how the atoms are *interconnected*, and therefore, does not have the notion of molecules and does not reflect it for a reader to see. Solidity programs may *not* lack functionality, but the Solidity AST will only talk of O and H, and not of H_2O, as the Lexon AST does. The connection of O and H would exist *implicitly* in the Solidity program. But in the Lexon AST, in this metaphor, the H_2O molecule would be spelled out explicitly.

Thus, because of the high level that Lexon has as a language, the 'meaning' of text written in Lexon is captured in Lexon's AST in a way *not* present in the AST of a lower level language.

This does not make Lexon AI but it does add something new that carries quite far.

Artificial Intelligence Tooling

"Machines will be capable, within twenty years, of doing any work a man can do."

Herbert A. Simon in 1956

While Lexon is no attempt at sentience, it owes its capabilities to using the models and tools developed for strong AI.[98] In fairness, all modern program languages do that, but Lexon uses them in a back-to-thee-roots style.

Lexon's approach might be regarded as 'coming full circle,' because ASTs are created by programs (compilers are themselves programs) that implement grammars that are defined using a notation called BNF[99] that was invented to describe the grammar of programming languages, and which was based on the Context Free Grammar (CFG)[100] popularized by the linguist Noam Chomsky. From right to left:

$$CFG \rightarrow BNF \rightarrow grammar \rightarrow compiler \rightarrow AST$$

Fig 31 – From Context Free Grammar to Abstract Syntax Tree

The linguistic research this came out of was in fact machine-oriented as his MIT work in the day was financed by the DoD in the hopes to produce natural speech-guided weapons

---

[98] Strong AI was the hope of researchers in the 50s, 60s and 80s that artificial general intelligence would be achievable.

[99] Backus-Naur Form – "a notation technique for context-free grammars, often used to describe the syntax of languages used in computing, such as computer programming languages, document formats, instruction sets and communication protocols. They are applied wherever exact descriptions of languages are needed" – https://en.wikipedia.org/wiki/Backus–Naur_form

[100] https://en.wikipedia.org/wiki/Context-free_grammar

systems.[101] Context Free Grammar was invented to describe and understand e.g. English better but was instead very successfully used to create a notation, BNF, that became the standard to describe the grammars of program languages, first among them ALGOL in 1960.[102]

As for linguistics, Context Free Grammars turned out to be *not* powerful enough to describe natural languages and the space moved on. Chomsky has long left this approach behind. No speech-controlled weapons systems were developed either, which is interesting, too. Did the research not work out? But in computer sciences, the model of Context Free Grammar thrived. BNF is in use for 60 years now to express the grammars of languages of the '3rd generation' – the likes of C, C++, Java – but also for the more logic-leaning languages like Lisp and Prolog that had once the hopes for strong AI riding on them.

Lexon applies Context Free Grammar, in the form of BNF, *back* to *natural* language, where the model came from, to create a program language in the intersection of what is expressible in natural language and what is parseable by a machine. So that a program can be expressed in a way that reads as easy as

---

[101] "Anthony Debons, a colonel in the United States Air Force, said, 'much of the research conducted at MIT by Chomsky and his colleagues [has] direct application to the efforts undertaken by military scientists to develop ... languages for computer operations in military command and control systems.' Between 1963 and 1965 Chomsky consulted on a military-sponsored project 'to establish natural language as an operational language for command and control.' Quoting Debons, A (1971). Alt, F.; Rubinoff, M. (eds.). "Command and Control: Technology and Social Impact". Advances in Computers. New York: Academic Press. 11: pg. 354 // and Newell, A. (1968). Bugliarello, George (ed.). Bioengineering: An Engineering View. Proceedings of a Symposium on the Engineering Significance of the Biological Sciences. San Francisco. pg. 271.
https://en.wikipedia.org/wiki/Noam_Chomsky
[102] Wikipedia speculates that Backus must have been familiar with Chomsky's work but note that Chomsky researched mechanical translation in his early days at the MIT in the mid 50s, before describing CFG. It is not entirely clear that the inspiration could not have flown the other way around, too.

natural language but can also be conveniently processed by a computer.

A More Elegant Stack

Regarding natural language processing, Lexon's approach cancels out the *layer of the computer language* itself. Because originally,

> (1st layer) **BNF** would be

> (2nd layer) used to define a language like **Lisp**

> (3rd layer) that would then be used to **program AI**, in Lisp

> (4th layer) that would process **natural language.**

The notion being that *thought* is something behind language, separate from it, hopefully captured on the 3rd level.

In other words, In the standard approach to AI in the 70s, the processing of natural language would have been the subject of the program programmed in Lisp, the 3rd level.

Lexon does not go for sentience and does not try to capture thought in analyzed form on the 3rd level, but uses natural language more directly, one layer deeper. With Lexon, it is the grammar of Lexon itself where natural language comes into play.

> (1st layer) **BNF** is used to

> (2nd layer) define controlled natural language i.e. **Lexon**

> (3rd layer) to write digital contracts in **natural language**.

There is no notion of AI, but natural language grammar is pervasive, reigning across all three layers. Because BNF itself was modelled on CFG that were invented to describe *human languages*. While it may not be the path to machine awareness, this is useful.

With Lexon, the place of natural language is directly adjacent to BNF, i.e. supported directly by the tool modeled on Context Free Grammar, instead of using BNF to build a non-natural language that then is used to program a program to process natural language.

For who has the taste for it, this is a more elegant and promising stack. With Lexon, 'meaning' is processed on the level comparable to the Lisp program code, instead of its runtime data. It drops the idea to separate intelligence and language and to express thought in anything else than natural language, unreflectedly. It doesn't try to have magic operating 'behind' the language, expressed in math.

This touches on a deep and controversial question of linguistics: is there, for humans, a neutral representation of reason 'behind' language? One that can intuitively be imagined to be the common well of speech no matter in what language a polyglot expresses herself? Leibniz thought so but didn't find much. Humboldt felt that thought could only exist in language and Loglan was invented by James Brown to find out if a better language would allow for better thought (pg. 354). Orwell had no doubt that language was needed for thinking (pg. 352) to the degree that degrading language could make thinking impossible. Chomsky subscribed to the hypothesis that an innate faculty of speech existed that would then give rise to language, but later moved away from this view.

Leibniz specifically proposed his *characteristica universalis* (pg. 105) as a necessary symbolism that would have to be discovered first, to express pure reason in it, cleaned of the peculiarities of natural language, so that one could automate reasoning. Suffice it to say that linguists cannot agree and the 20th century saw a back and forth. In so far as strong AI research in the 70s very much assumed that sentience should be achievable on a more mathematical level than language, Lexon is a late but timely complement to that, mirroring the more neglected half of linguistic research, which posits that thought might not be separable from language.

Preservation Instead of Decomposition

This may provide an alternative answer to the 70s quest to find a manageable way to have programs *self-modify*[103] – something that inevitably makes programs impossible to debug and was therefore abandoned, if with a heavy heart. Self-modification looked promising because the thinking went: for it to be AI, *something more* than what the programmers put *in* would have to come *out*. Not just more numbers or words but more insight, more logic. In that light, what would be more plausible than to suspect this 'more' to be found in newly, self-created code. If the third level (pg. 146), the Lisp program, could 'reflect' upon itself and modify itself even, it could perhaps produce emergent results on level 4. This was an attempt to break through the limitations of the standard von Neumann architecture of computers that separates code from data, i.e. the program from its subject.

Lexon follows a different path: it *steps out of the way*. It does not add anything, but instead preserves the structure of the input so well that the output has stronger semblance to human communication. The translation step is cut out that went from input into meaning and back – i.e. from language to math back to language. There is still processing, a transformation from input to output. But no attempt to transform thought and logic, expressed in human language, into its condensed essence and back. No attempt, that is, to create 'intelligence.' But in so far as a program takes human input to produce meaningful results, Lexon can *transport* more of the human-understandable mesh of meaning from input to output, *intact*. This has practical benefits ranging from improved communication about code, when writing it; over the long-elusive price of self-documentation; to a quantum leap in front-end generation and literally involving different parts of the brain in programming.

---

[103] For an example, see FLOW-MATIC, pg. 297, line 12. This was not programmed in a self-modifying way to create AI though but to save space.

Controlled Language

Throughout, Lexon code lives on a very high level: the example of Fig 22, pg. 132 – **Signer certifies Data** – expresses that someone should digitally sign some data, without at that point caring about who or what. In other languages this is a fringe case that will routinely require many lines of code. Which illustrates how a Lexon program is much closer to real-world people, and their actions, as its subject that is reasoned about.

The focus on this high level of the language results into this high-level AST. Or, flipping it around, designing for such high-level AST is what enabled such a high-level language.

This approach is called *controlled natural language*: not the attempt to parse just *any* legal text – i.e. *not* to try Natural Language Processing, the ultimate dream of Computational Law – but instead, to require a *subset of natural language* grammar as the language that the legal contract must be written in. A subset that can then with reasonable effort be processed with very conventional compiler build tools.

This approach turned out to be more powerful than imagined.

Meaning

ASTs of complex programs can easily consist of millions of nodes; but only in a casual sense can it be said that an AST hold 'meaning.' An AST will *reflect* meaning, to a lesser or higher degree and it can certainly be used to create output that is based on the meaning that it reflects, the AST serving as conduit. The 'signified' that is 'meant' may not be present, but its *structure* is, and this is enough for production.

The AST, describing *relationships* in its edges, could be seen as the meta data of the signified. As is well understood today, this can often be more powerful than the actual data.

Metadata instead of Meaning

E.g. an AST has no notion at all what a 'buyer' is and the actual *name* of a definition (e.g. the text string "**Buyer**" itself) is routinely *stripped out* of the information that goes into an AST, because the machine has no use for it. There is no sentience in an AST to which this name would mean anything. However, the AST reflects an arbitrary entity's *relationships* with *some other* entity and the rights and options those entities have against each other. This may actually be the more relevant aspect of the notion of what a 'buyer' is; more relevant than the name "**Buyer!**"

Because, the abstract notion of a 'buyer' will be understood slightly different by any thinker. The idea that there is one abstract image of a buyer that everyone shares is a simplification that is not too helpful but quite obscuring, and points to the core of every honest dispute over agreements where people thought they understood each other but they didn't.

The reality is that there are myriads of different, private associations in billions of brains across the globe that are associated with the word 'buyer.' You'd be lucky to rely on a common understanding of the word and not get into a dispute over an honest misunderstanding.

In that light, it is more useful to have a precisely defined pattern – the edges in the AST – that describe *one specific* buyer, the one and only that is meant by the specific contract in question that the AST describes. The specificness renders obsolete the role that the inexact and blurry name "**Buyer**" could play. The actual functionality of the contract is the better description of exactly *that* 'buyer' that is meant in the specific instance. It doesn't matter either if the 'buyer' is also a 'payer' etc. These categories are all replaced by the very specific rights the Lexon code bestows.

Obviously, this reflects how legal contracts work today: they use words like 'buyer' but define them more precisely as capitalized "Buyer", a term then understood to be one specific person and *not* meaning all possible 'buyers.' The entire contract being but the listing of the actual rights and obligations of that person without relying on the original meaning of the word. Clarifications will even be provided as to what this specific **Buyer** may *not* be entitled to that the word 'buyer' may otherwise imply. At which point confusion of 'buyer' and 'Buyer' might have problematic consequences and it might as well be better if a different term than 'buyer' was used, e.g. "Party 1". Or no word at all – as is the case in Lexon's 'brain.'

Lexon as AI (not)

Looking deeper into the meaning of 'meaning' can lead to the case that Lexon is, in fact, AI. This is not what we claim but the exercise is instructive. This taps into an ancient flame war.

There is not a lot of consensus now but until about 400 years ago, the term 'meaning' was commonly understood as something that is pointed to. In the sense that a sign means something, as does a word, as well as a name and a symbol.

But like a 'Pegasus,' what is pointed to, does not necessarily have to exist.

Aristotle calls that something the 'essence', which cannot be predicated of anything else.[104] The Lexon AST does not *contain* this essence, it only points to it. But this is true as well for words and texts: they can point to meaning but *are* not the essence themselves. Because the essence is held to exist independently of the words and explanations describing it. And many words in many languages are thought by many to point to the same essence.[105]

Talking about AI, the question becomes what our brains are. Technically, they are pattern processors of a power far superior to current computer hardware: the cortex alone has 16 billion parallel cores, as opposed to 10 million that the most parallelized super computer fields today.[106] It is fair to assume that such processing power can create convincing emergent effects. And we are 7 billion, heavily interacting.

But Aristotle it seems would not have claimed that our brains contain essence either. Our thoughts, when we think in words, only point to it, like a document.[107] Which means that the Lexon AST, in so far as it reflects meaning – or essence – does the same as our brains. It operates on symbols. Hopefully logically. It does not contain the essence; it just processes the pointers to it. This can be said of any program. But Lexon programs will produce output that is more familiar to our brain processing, as it leaves the structure intact that we use, and processes a subset of the protocol we apply: natural language.

Extreme Constructivism of course claims that there is not actually anything that is pointed to, no essence, and that

---

[104] https://plato.stanford.edu/entries/aristotle-metaphysics/

[105] On the exploration of the relationship between language and thinking, see Appendix IV: Constructed Human Languages, from pg. 309.

[106] https://en.wikipedia.org/wiki/Sunway_TaihuLight

[107] Although I fully believe Rick Dudley that he could think before he could speak or think in words.

the reference patterns that our thoughts are, only ever refer to each other. What is pointed to, the meaning, was itself only pointers. On that premise, the Lexon AST could then be said to hold meaning proper.

> "The term 'theory of meaning' has figured, in one way or another, in a great number of philosophical disputes over the last century. Unfortunately, this term has also been used to mean a great number of different things. … it is worth noting that one prominent tradition in the philosophy of language denies that there are facts about the meanings of linguistic expressions."[108]

Let's say 'meaning' in this context, deserves quotes.

---

[108] https://plato.stanford.edu/entries/meaning/

SCOPE OF APPLICATION

"In considering any new subject, there is frequently a tendency, first, to overrate what we find to be already interesting or remarkable; and, secondly, by a sort of natural reaction, to undervalue the true state of the case, when we do discover that our notions have surpassed those that were really tenable."

Ada Lovelace[109]

When legal professionals are excited about the possibilities of Lexon, they are really excited about the possibilities that arise from a legal contract being truthfully captured as AST. The part of the 'meaning' of a contract that Lexon captures is the part that matters for automation.

As described above, while Lexon does not capture the meaning of defined *names*, it does understand their express *relationships*. And Lexon *does* 'understand' a number of verbs.

The following is a discussion of technical and functional aspects that illustrate the reach that Lexon is soon to develop.

---

[109] Note G, 1842

Output & Portability

Solidity & Sophia

The Lexon compiler right now creates Ethereum Solidity smart contracts and Aeternity Sophia smart contracts from Lexon code. More target platforms will be added in the future, including for JavaScript, i.e. off-chain processing of contracts.

WebAssembly

The compiler can be built to WebAssembly (WASM), which gives Lexon online editors a powerful, local install feel and is the route to integration path e.g. with Polkadot Substrate Parachains.[110] The WASM build is used in the three online editors at http://demo.lexon.tech, https://remix.ethereum.org and https://fire.aeternity.com.

Off-chain

We are also working on a stand-alone interpreter that will allow Lexon code to be run independently of blockchains. This is interesting for virtual sidechain scenarios that use conventional full stack technology but write away hashes of their results to a blockchain.

Prose & Glossary

The Lexon compiler from the start also created 'even more human readable contract prose' from Lexon code. This will be

---

[110] https://polkadot.network/build

amended with a detailed, automatic glossary for every relevant English word used in the contract.

Contract Management

The AST is used to generate input screens and runtime monitor apps for the blockchain representation of a contract that show how it changes state and that allow to interact with the contract automation in the most elegant way. Significantly more productive user interfaces can be generated by using the high-level information that Lexon code contains, than when the starting point is 3rd generation code like Solidity.

Multi-Lingual and Multi-Jurisdictional Code

Multilingual Code

The Lexon compiler will process *different natural languages*, like German and Spanish. We tested Japanese successfully and will trial Dutch next.

Jurisdictions

Lexon will feature automatisms to incorporate different jurisdictions. By a standard concept known as *object frameworks* in programming, different terms will acquire different meaning, depending on context.

Domains

A similar extension mechanism will allow to define new native verbs for Lexon, e.g. 'move' for robotics or 'format' for output.

Analysis

Visualization

We are working on visualization tools that will allow for visual programming and for the creation of a visual depiction of a contract's logic. Because Lexon 'understands' the contract code to some degree, it can support the legal engineer by reflecting back what the logic of a contract is, in the form of a chart.

Automated Tests

The Lexon AST can be used for *software test processes* to test the (legal) completeness of the code (loopholes etc.), as well as if it results in implausible results for any possible input. One such procedure is called *Monte Carlo simulation*: the contract can be bombarded with millions of different events, to see under which circumstances, if any, it would produce implausible results.

Decision Making

Simulation of Lexon code can *automate the decision making* of a judge. Any smart contract could do that, but smart contracts are almost never *digitally expressed*. This is not the same as when a program is just the *representation* of a contract. Blockchain smart contracts today do some things automatically but are removed at least one full degree from being the direct expression of the *meeting of the minds* that a judge will look for as 'the contract'. Because Lexon code *is* that legally enforceable contract itself, the automatic decisions that can be calculated based on its AST are of a different quality. This might seem subtle but actually is not. Especially when a contract is complex and the history of the case long, a huge amount of fact-finding and learning about the minutiae of a case falls by the way side when Lexon code is used, which will result in much fairer results because it reduces the influence of money: i.e. to be able to pay for long hours, or to buy the more renown or skilled story teller to argue a more convincing story in court when facts are just too complex to understand and argue.

Expected Value

The AST can also be used to calculate the *Expected Value* of a contract, a single number that businesspeople produce by assigning probabilities and results to different possible outcomes. This today is slow and error prone, the AST can do it 'for free' and without fail. The gain of exactitude and speed is achieved in the same way as described before: the process of creating a mathematical model that describes the contract can simply be skipped.

DOMAINS OF APPLICATION

Lexon's usefulness is anchored in the intersection of the blockchain and the legal sphere and extends far beyond.

Regarding trustless technology, the fascination with Lexon is by no means restricted to the legal domain: many efforts benefit from having the algorithms at the heart of their implementation being readable to everyone involved, programmer or not. Legally vetted or not.[111]

But Lexon is useful no matter who provides for the trust. i.e. a blockchain or not. The reality of many industries today is that they have long established trusted third parties installed that take care of interests of the entire industry or facilitate key functions for an entire domain. Even if these trusted third parties do not plan on replacing themselves by a blockchain, they might benefit from making their automated processes more transparent by programming them in Lexon. As a first step towards becoming a blockchain-based service or as a completely independent effort.

The following is a list if areas where Lexon will be of help.

---

[111] A major concern of CAOLA is that regulators might strangle the new possibilities of blockchains before they can even be researched, much less demonstrated. There are many projects that are by no means criminal, neither in spirit nor in practice but have not figured out their path to compliance. Lexon helps to ask the right questions as it highlights problems and allows to pull in lawyers in a much more productive way.

Private Contracting Long Tail

Lexon might facilitate legal literacy to become common place. Normal people are empowered to create and manage their own contracts, potentially often for cases where in the past it was understood that the overhead of a contract would have been too expensive. Lawyers may find additional business being asked for guidance in this extended realm of application of private law.

Terms of Service

Lexon might help end the issue of terms of services that everyone knows no one reads. Because Lexon code can be processed electronically, terms of service that are articulated in Lexon can be matched against a potential customer's personal limits and demands. This has been tried before in regard to privacy on the web but failed, potentially because a bespoke protocol had been developed for it. TOS written in Lexon will not require any additional effort to understand: the text of the TOS would *not* need a technical companion file or anything like it. Once the potential is understood, lawmakers might require businesses to use Lexon to articulate their TOS, at least on the web.

Decentralized Autonomous Organizations

Lexon signifies a quantum leap for DAOs because it can unify the legal and the blockchain rules that govern them. A Lexon charta for a cooperative can in some jurisdiction be turned into a legal person by the act of deploying it to the blockchain: giving a DAO legal personhood:[112] the power to legally own and deal in real world assets and legally shield members who could otherwise, by default, be exposed to full private liability for the DAO's actions. Contracts that this DAO closes with anyone can then likewise be real contracts before the law. At the very least, writing a DAO's code in Lexon will help to make sure that the blockchain code is compliant with existing laws and regulation and makes the rules transparent for all members.

AI Safety & Data Protection

Lexon should be the language that lawmakers use to articulate the Robotic Laws[113] in that we need now. The advantage of using Lexon is that hardware producers can be obliged *to build in the very code* that the lawmakers created. The law itself, verbatim, then *is* program code. The room for honest and dishonest mistakes is eliminated that usually separates the patient letters of a law from its implementation. By the same token, data protection algorithms can be made transparent and mandatory for social media and data processing organizations, public and private. This may be the most important application of Lexon.

Trade

A natural talent of Lexon is any form of trade. This is the classic blockchain case, but adding readability of the contracts, which

---

[112] Only a person can own things. Human beings are 'natural persons,' while companies and communities are 'legal persons.'
[113] See footnote 14 on pg. 11

might be the missing link to convince companies to realize the cost, speed and reliability advantages of blockchain smart contracts and crypto payments.

Ex-Ante Regulation

Regulations are more specific than laws and to the degree that they deal in concrete procedures, measurements and formulas, they can be expressed in Lexon code. Using 'libraries', regulators will be able to craft Lexon code that will allow businesses to create contracts for themselves that will be compliant by construction: by including the regulators' code in their contracts, the proceedings are guaranteed to comply with such regulations.

RegTech & Oversight

In RegTech, blockchains disintermediate the auditors' *supervisors* first. They don't necessarily put auditors out of business. For example, in a study for the European Commission the result pointed to bank auditors' *supervisors* being replaced by a blockchain concept, not the auditors themselves. When push comes to shove someone still has to check that a hash and a dataset really belong together.

For all the possibilities that blockchains used *as timestamping service* offer for regulation, few have so far been used. Lexon might change this because it shortens the decision process for lawmakers and regulators who might have dragged their feet in the face of the unknown unknowns of the new technology. The guarantees that Lexon code extends are much easier to understand, discuss and adjust to.

Law

Lexon might even be used as language of law. This was not a design goal, but it was suspected that Lexon might beat the path, first from smart contracts to legal contracts, then on to regulations and in due course help find the gate to the auto-mation of law. The first step happened with Carla Reyes' exam-ple for the UCC Financial Statement (pg. 79) that illustrates how using Lexon might improve legal code and provide for a path to improve legislation that is unprecedented. This works for the UCC chapter 9 form because the law in this case is very proce-dural. That is not a rare exception though, as many statutes are very concrete and could as such be re-articulated in Lexon. Law reforms are not a frequent thing and we are suddenly talking about a 100-year horizon now. But things should accelerate once the benefits are understood.

The likely path here is that lawmakers would for a start explicitly ok agencies' use of Lexon to re-articulate procedures to automate them in an economic and transparent way. It might then become obvious that this kind of automation could be the text of the law in the first place.

Our current research seems to also have unearthed the path yet higher up the abstraction levels, beyond relatively pro-cedural statutes to more general ones (see pg. 120).

Governance

Lexon is a dream for all initiatives that care about improvement of governance, e.g. of existing cooperatives, using blockchain or not. Lexon allows to articulate the rules in clear language and then provides certainty that they can be performed without fail. Smart contracts can reduce overhead and costs for every single community that governs itself. Their 'trustless' aspects –

when using a blockchain – help prevent opportunity for graft and breach of trust. But Lexon code may just as well be run off-chain to demonstrate that the rules stated in the charta are applied as intended. For blockchain-centric communities, Lexon closes a gap that until now existed in the trustless world: that everyone still had to trust the programmers that smart contracts did what the programmers said they would.

Bills of Exchange

Bills of Exchange are a prominent example of a powerful, existing legal framework that is currently not used much, but still on the books and a potential blockchain killer app in-waiting. BoEs were in use for over a thousand years, they became obsolete only recently due to electronic money transfer and credit cards. The specialty of BoEs is how they invert the burden of proof to seize someone's bank account. After a BoE matures there is no further process required. Lexon allows for a BoE to be spelled out as legally required, and at the same time managed on-chain. On maturity they might double as facilitator of a cryptocurrency payment or serve as proof to a bank that a payment is due.

Financial Instruments & DeFi

For any type of financial instrument, Lexon enhances the revolutionary capabilities of blockchain with its trademark complete congruence of legal contracting and automation. It will hold for Wallstreet like for Mainstreet that people will be much more open to a new technology when it can be made accessible in the way that Lexon makes blockchain smart contracts transparent for all involved. This may help to tap the unrealized potential of blockchain as a transparent platform for bearer assets, with all the risk reduction this entails. A major development that will benefit from the availability of Lexon are liquidity-assured CDOs that have direct access to their slice of the collateral, using digital assets and token mechanisms, even through multiple steps of securitization. Lexon will make these complex instruments safer by making them readable.

Provenance

OpenSC[114] proposes a protocol for proving the eco claims that underly eco seals. They will use Lexon – off-chain in the instance – to process environmental data, e.g. satellite imagery, that is inspected to satisfy requirements as set forth in the code, e.g. that a forest line at a given geo coordinate has not changed. The advantage of using Lexon for the central piece of processing is that it makes the claim understandable for anyone without any aspect left where a consumer who is not themselves a programmer would have to trust – even just trust that the programmers did not make an honest mistake.

Academic Certification

Badges and Micro-Credentialing will change education and HR in the coming decade. The basic premise is that former university students will be able to give finer-grained proof of their specific preparations for an employment they might be applying for. It's obvious how such a system should be implemented on a blockchain network and how it would benefit from being programmed in Lexon so that the entire process is completely

---

[114] OpenSC – https://opensc.org

transparent. Note that technically, credentials can be realized by simple digital signatures. A blockchain system, however, allows for corrections and, in the blockchain itself, provides the ubiquitous, always available storage platform for the badges.

Supply Chain & Trade Finance

Supply chains remain a giant blockchain play even though current flagship efforts like by IBM[115] and Maersk may not be progressing as swiftly as anticipated. The real promise is in how procurement and nested sub-contracting can be automated and by this made safer, faster, more reliable and much less costly. This is a matter of interfaces and conventions being established in the spirit of ERC[116] standards, so that smart contracts can interact across the blockchain that is their common platform. Lexon will increase the circle of people who can actively shape these ecosystems and need to make informed decisions to move the status quo forward without endangering their business.

Logistics & Ride-Sharing

The real promise of ride-sharing has not been realized. It lies in a more grass-roots version of neighborhood self-help. The fact is that a massive number of cars ride the same routes every day. The number of unused seats and cargo space is relatively predictable and the gigantic effort to implement carpool lanes is

---

[115] TradeLens – https://blog.tradelens.com/news/building-apis-for-shipping-what-weve-learned-so-far
[116] ERCs are those Ethereum Improvement Proposals that deal in application-level standards and conventions – https://eips.ethereum.org/erc

an indicator of how high the value is estimated to be that is lying untapped in a more effective organization of people's commute. Importantly also for the environment. Novel business models that are less cynical than Uber are banking on blockchain technology and tokens to propose the next, greener and more economic phase in mobility. Lexon will be part of this second phase and the B2B aspects of this development, where more bespoke agreements are needed, sometimes ad hoc, but with the capacity to be plugged into blockchain-based logistics platforms.

Future-Proofing

It is not clear which blockchain will succeed to solve today's scalability and privacy challenges, but Lexon's versatility makes investment into smart programming future-proof. No matter which platform will be the main network in the future, Lexon will be able to compile Lexon code to it. Or if for other reasons it becomes desirable to switch from one platform to another, Lexon makes it possible to do so with minimal disruption. This on top of the fact that Lexon code – because of how clear it is – reduces the risk of lock-in by programmers.

Escrow

As shown in our very first example (pg. 3), escrow is a home game for Lexon. This is a classic blockchain strength, Lexon merely democratizes the tool and gives it into the hands of anyone who is interested to use blockchain technology, without the need to consult with a programmer to implement the desired functionality. But at the same time without limits on fine-tuning the contract to exactly what the desired functionality is.

Minor differences in the code can have a major effect with escrow contracts. Lexon allows full freedom to articulate constraints and options exactly as needed.

Wills

Last wills are another classic blockchain example that requires maximal trust in what a smart contract actually says. In the end they are but a special form of escrow. Wills might never become big business, but the advent of stable coins is what makes them interesting beyond crypto-maximalist. Writing a blockchain will in Lexon might become a commodity service, as it is so simple that a notary might offer it as value-add. There might not even be a change in how the industry works in this regard today. But this is less likely to come true as long as smart contracts require a programmer or that you trust a third-party app that creates the contract for you.

Wills will not be restricted to crypto assets. Any ownership transfer will be possible based on the certified result of a blockchain algorithm: a smart contract that expresses a Will may be foremost busy with keeping track of events and providing what the desired outcome would be given those events.

Crowdfunding

Using Lexon for crowdfunding includes all non-programmers interested in funding a project into the group of people who can understand how the smart contract works that they are asked to send money to. Lexon will allow to craft more bespoke agreements, better suited to an individual project than the cookie cutter contracts that we are used to today.

Mutual and Retail Insurance

The reason you cannot insure your party against weather events today is that this type of insurance is not commercially interesting for insurers. Weather insurance is difficult to get even for farmers who depend on the weather for their livelihoods. Lexon should help to create mutual insurances that work with trusted oracles – e.g. to decide about payouts for bad weather. This has always been a blockchain mainstay example but Lexon takes out the intransparency of current smart contract languages to include non-nerds. This can allow for costs to come down and a critical mass of participants in the market to be reached so that either mutual insurance becomes viable or insurance companies come on board. Lexon will also make the required legal research many times easier: to find out what legal form would be required for such an insurance. And Lexon would allow for readability of the charta of a DAO that might run the insurance pool, making it a real legal person.

Information Sale and Sharing

The future of blockchains might be the sale of information. The most important functionality of smart contracts might soon be to grant or refuse access to well defined portions of data. This is not possible today with most platforms as they cannot store secrets or secret keys. But this is changing and, in the future, the 'new oil' should become the main digital good that blockchains manage and provide access to, for a fee. Lexon will enable lawmakers to chime in – using ex-ante regulation – to protect consumers and will allow customers to express their precise interest and limits. The tangle of conditions that can be expected to be articulated by consumers, will probably be much safer and much clearer when programmed in Lexon – which has the right abstraction level – than any other language.

Digital Asset Markets

A major motivation to create Lexon was to 'synchronize the shift of possession and ownership.' The thinking goes that the magic of blockchain tech is, that programs can transfer money in an unstoppable way. The one recourse though that anyone always has is to sue. The best dis-incentive against someone going to court for corrupt motives will be that a smart contract is human-readable, for the judge to find out immediately that what happened on the chain *was* exactly as agreed. This basic premise holds for all valuables that may change hands on a blockchain: the trade will be safer when the smart contracts behind it can be presented to a judge. It will reduce the likeliness to be sued. All other advantages for non-programmers of course also apply.

The diversity of uses is apparent. The accuracy of Lexon's abstraction process provides for the breadth of its applicability.

The expectation is that a multitude of relevant application domains will be added to this list. This is because Lexon's AST comes so close to expressing the actual meaning of a contract; while contracts are used and looked at in so many different ways. All of which Lexon captures – or rather: leaves intact.

In the end, Lexon improves any blockchain use case and might help to get it into production. It can make many legal procedures faster, more economic and transparent.

And it may be used for programs that have nothing to do with any of the above but will just benefit from readability for all stakeholders.

MOTIVATION

To give an idea where we might be headed, here is a personal account on how Lexon came about.

Lexon started as an idea about how to make smart contracts safer to use. The magic of blockchains is that programs send money, directly. If you saw the backends of mobile payment you'd appreciate what a transformative power that is. One of the early visions was that of IoT devices becoming economically autonomous. But the *change of possession* that smart contract can effect could still be challenged in court. The argument would go that a smart contract didn't work as expected. This would be difficult to disprove, and potentially costly every single time.

But if smart contracts could be readable by a judge, the refutation of frivolous claims would be so much easier, it would nearly eliminate any incentive to go to court with a made-up claim. By means of 'human-readability' Lexon was to add the reliable change of *ownership* to go with the change of possession that blockchains facilitate.

When I wrote the book on Ethereum, I wrote a paragraph about the idea of Ethereum smart contracts in natural English, fully convinced that projects existed that worked on it. The idea was in the air in 2016 and it seemed just a matter of time. But I found out I was wrong, no one was working on it, I had to revise that paragraph. I started asking around and learned that despite the fact that numerous languages had been created for Ethereum at this point, the vision of human-readability was seen as a challenge of a different magnitude. I found it tempting because I had created a complete suite of tools for a domain specific language (DSL) and virtual machine with unusual features before, for the insurance industry. There was no question that everyone loved the idea and it would have viral potential. It would be a really good thing to have, it just wasn't happening. This started to look like it was on me.

I used Christmas 2016 to sit down and prove out the basic premise, coming up with a first working demo that could compile a minimal 'human-readable' example contract. I started to look for partners and late summer the next year had the opportunity to find feedback from Oliver Goodenough and Carla Reyes for the first Lexon whitepaper. My closest confidant from the start was TJ Saw, a lawyer and entrepreneur who had practiced trade law and created software to find loopholes in (natural language) contracts, together with Gavin Wood, the co-founder of Ethereum. On the technical side, MIT's Thomas Hardjono played an important role for me, a crypto and open source veteran who had shepherded the Kerberos Consortium, a crucial contribution to secure communication.

In 2018 the formation of the Lexon Foundation was announced in Davos, angel money raised and the core of the Lexon community assembled, 70 experts across the different fields that the vision touched upon. Over the course of 2019 we created Lexon 0.2 and collected feedback at conferences all over the world. By that year the design had evolved to something better than I had expected to be possible, thanks to the push from Open Source legend Brian Fox. I had not thought that readability without *any* learning curve, without any preparational study of programming really, would be possible. The price for it, lower writeability, looked forbidding. But it turned out to be the fiery dust that made Lexon come into its own.

It also became apparent that half of the work to make Lexon fly would be communication. It was just too far out; the vision communicates in seconds, but people would not necessarily dare to trust their intuition about possibilities even after seeing a live demo. And while there was a good deal of alchemistic creativity required in the design of the language, the material deliverable turned out to be the cross-sectional communication with lawyers and business people to find, word by word, what it would take to make the language feel at home to them.

It was exceedingly difficult to get guidance out of lawyers, and almost impossible without specific examples as starting point of a discussion. Lexon evolved deploying the Stone method to the extreme: programming something that might hit it, showing it to people and see how they react, then going back and iterate to get closer the next time. Unsurprisingly, I had to unlearn my take on code as a life-long programmer. It was a revelation to discover how different non-coders intuit the meaning of code, how right they can be, how off, how blind-folded by arbitrary convention we programmers. Of course, the goal was always to make Lexon look and feel simple, and we are succeeding. Lexon will hopefully appear as an 'obvious' de-sign – and never betray how incredibly hard it was to source direction.

In mid 2019 it became clear that Lexon was unique be-yond the narrow confines of the blockchain world. I had until that point discouraged everyone from even exploring this question. But now there is demand for an off-chain version of Lexon that could process Lexon code trust-fully, e.g. for pro-cessing contracts in-house. It also turned out that there is inter-est in Lexon for its readability alone, independent of legal ques-tions, e.g. for communities creating DAOs. The course was held steady in 2019 to avoid death by feature creep but plans for 2020 were adapted accordingly.

Throughout, there is the question, what Lexon is. How it achieves what it does, and also to what extent it is actually new. There were genuine inventions made to get where we are: e.g. one insight is that non-programmers often do understand ab-stractions perfectly well, but only un-nested and only without the burden of the overhead of giving the principle a name: in-stead staying with exactly one level of abstraction and concrete examples. Lexon yields to this finding in multiple aspects and that is one factor that makes it different from other programming languages. It's a simple limitation, but the consequences are substantial.

On the other hand, Lexon is also based on advanced programming techniques that are not familiar to the majority of programmers, which has resulted into some voicing doubts that it could actually work, even after being shown real, working code.[117] The prime example here is how Lexon employs pattern matching that is borrowed from functional languages. Lexon mixes higher-order logic in, to, in a very pragmatic way, attach itself to the idiosyncrasies of smart contracts and allow for code that reads more like natural prose – in the instance, to be able to introduce names without any context. No magic there, no rocket science either, it's just different, serves the purpose – and irritates programmers.

And so, from the start, there has been enthusiasm for the vision of human-readable smart contracts by a select few, who carried the development. And the circle of pioneers who love it is widening, some have tried their hand at the idea themselves before finding Lexon. Mind-bending moments of insights happen thanks to experts in the fields giving their view and support.

But generally, neither lawyers nor programmers develop a crush on Lexon at first sight. In the real world, seasoned practitioners of law have no time for claims of disruption of their 3,000-year-old profession. Worse, lawyers are just no fans of stuff like programming. There are jokes amongst them, I learned, that essentially go 'Oh, sure, I too had no talent for STEM but still wanted to go to university. So, chose law.' This, self-deprecating humor does not instill courage to try coding.[118]

---

[117] Most devs crack a sibylline smile when they see Lexon for the first time.

[118] Luka Müller, whose lawfirm guided Ethereum to regulatory safety in Switzerland, laughed when he first saw Lexon and said, "yes, lawyers won't like it, but their bosses will make them use it."

There are also enough conservative programmers who don't appreciate anything that doesn't look like ALGOL and don't program on weekends or at night. Lexon is not the first and will not be the last programming language to be criticized simply for looking unusual. Ironically, by lowering the threshold for everyone else, Lexon raises it for programmers. It's like learning a language that is similar to one you know: there is a constant danger of making wrong assumptions.

That's why we are working to prove Lexon top-down. A big bang event will be necessary where a flagship project using Lexon will make the world take note and start thinking about what might just have become possible. This will make people more confident to give it a shot themselves and maybe proposed it as an option at their corporate home. To that end, we are working with deciders and C-level management to realize reference implementations of big global brands using Lexon. At the same time, we are going into the universities to help to create the first Lexon curriculums to reach the next generation of lawyers. To train the first legal engineers.

Consider deploying your first digital contract now if you have not already done so, at **http://demo.lexon.tech.** Use an example, try changing it a little bit right in your browser, deploy and manage it, to get a first-hand impression of how accessible blockchain smart contracts can be.

Hopefully this will be just a beginning and we'll see you around.

It would be awesome to hear from you with feedback to lexon.bible@gmail.com or if you asked your questions on the mailing list that you can join at http://list.lexon.tech.

Thank you

REFERENCE

This reference may serve to give a first-hand impression about how Lexon works concretely. It is still in flux and best looked up online when the intent is to create real code.

http://lexon.tech/reference

. (THE DOT)

end of statements

<statement>.

<expression>.

The dot signifies the end of a statement or expression. It is explained with the respective grammar. It cannot be used as part of definition names or in any other function. The dot is usually also the end of a line.

Dots do not matter in COMMENTS.

GRAMMAR

This is a word that is part of the meta structure of Lexon code. It groups and gives meaning to the terms following it.

LEXON 0.1

EXAMPLE

"Grantor" is a person.

A

optional article to increase readability

FILLER

This is a filler that is ignored by the Lexon transpiler and virtusal machine. It can be ommitted with no change to script functionality. The legal prose output, however, could be affected.

EXAMPLE

"Grantor" is a person.

VARIANTS

AN

SYNONYMS

THE

LEXON 0.1

ABORTED
end the performance

PERFORMANCE

This term controls the performance of the code, e.g. if following statements apply, or not; or if the contract should terminate.

LEXON 0.2

EXAMPLE

And with this, the
Proposal is aborted.

AFTER

later in time

COMPARISON

This is an comparison operator to compare two values. It operates on names and literal values. Comparisons are used to assigned the binary result to names, to inform the performance of the code and to evaluate verification claims.

LEXON 0.3

EXAMPLE

The Due Date is set as the Delivery Time after the current time.

AFTERWARDS

conditional and chronological order

<statement>, and afterward
<statement>

indicates that the following statement should come into effect if the preceding was performed. If the preceding statement could not be performed, the following statement should not even be looked at.

SEQUENCE

This word puts statements before and after it in chronological order. This is a reserved keyword that has significant meaning to the Lexon transpiler and virtual machine. It cannot be used as a variable or contract name. It does not matter whether any of its letters are written in lower or upper case. Other words can include this keyword as part.

LEXON 0.2

EXAMPLE

and afterwards publish
Owner and Cost.

VARIANTS

AND AFTERWARDS

SYNONYMS

THEREBY, AND ALSO

ALSO

conditional and chronological order

also <provision>

SEQUENCE

This word puts statements before and after it in chronological order. This is a reserved keyword that has significant meaning to the Lexon transpiler and virtual machine. It cannot be used as a variable or contract name. It does not matter whether any of its letters are written in lower or upper case. Other words can include this keyword as part.

LEXON 0.2

EXAMPLE

Also provided that the Owner is not This Contract.

AMOUNT

a number

"<name>" is [an] amount.

This keyword is used to state that a name will mean a number, e.g. amounts of crypto currency.

TYPE

This is a type name, which is used to clarify what kind of data which name definition might stand for. A type name can be used like a definition, i.e. a name could be defined that has the same name like its type. But no definition may have the name of a type other than its own.

LEXON 0.1

EXAMPLE

"Inheritance" is an amount.

AMOUNT OF

optional indicator that the value and not the name is used for a calculation

FILLER

This is a filler that is ignored by the Lexon transpiler and virtusal machine. It can be ommitted with no change to script functionality. The legal prose output, however, could be affected.

LEXON 0.3

EXAMPLE

Increase the count of Votes by the amount of Nays.

AND

conditional and chronological order

`<binary> and <binary>`

`<statement> and <statement>`

And is used similar to its meaning in natural language, for concatenation of two or more instructions and also in conjunction with commas. Different to most other program languages, 'and' can allow to re-use a subject.

SEQUENCE

This word puts statements before and after it in chronological order. This is a reserved keyword that has significant meaning to the Lexon transpiler and virtual machine. It cannot be used as a variable or contract name. It does not matter whether any of its letters are written in lower or upper case. Other words can include this keyword as part.

LEXON 0.1

EXAMPLE

The Executor may pay the Escrow to the Heir and terminate this contract.

AND ALSO

conditional and chronological order

<statement> and also <statement>

indicates that the following statement should come into effect if the preceding was performed. If the preceding statement could not be performed, the following statement should not even be looked at.

Commas can be used to chain multiple statements together that are each understood to be temporally ordered by and also from the first to the last.

SEQUENCE

This word puts statements before and after it in chronological order. This is a reserved keyword that has significant meaning to the Lexon transpiler and virtual machine. It cannot be used as a variable or contract name. It does not matter whether any of its letters are written in lower or upper case. Other words can include this keyword as part.

EXAMPLE

The Payer pays an Amount into escrow, appoints the Payee, and also fixes the Fee.

SYNONYMS

THEREBY, AFTERWARDS

LEXON 0.2

AND WITH THIS

conditional and chronological order

<statement> and with this, <statement>

SEQUENCE

This word puts statements before and after it in chronological order. This is a reserved keyword that has significant meaning to the Lexon transpiler and virtual machine. It cannot be used as a variable or contract name. It does not matter whether any of its letters are written in lower or upper case. Other words can include this keyword as part.

LEXON 0.2

EXAMPLE

And with this, the Proposal is Aborted.

ANY

optional article to increase readability

FILLER

This is a filler that is ignored by the Lexon transpiler and virtual machine. It can be ommitted with no change to script functionality. The legal prose output, however, could be affected.

LEXON 0.3

EXAMPLE

Redefine the Possessor
to be any person.

ANYONE
blanket permission

anyone may <statement>

PERMISSION

This keyword allows to articulate who should be allowed to initiate the performance of a given clause.

LEXON 0.3

EXAMPLE

Anyone may: if Next Tax Due Date has passed, then:
Trigger The Default.

APPOINT

assign meaning to a name

<person> appoint[s] <person> to be
<person>.

Used to define the meaning of a name. Appoint works only for names that did not have a meaning assigned before. To change a name's meaning, use 'redefine' or 'change'.

Though it would not be sensible natural grammar, appoint can be used to define other than person names.

ASSIGNMENT

This term is used to define the value of a name.

VARIANTS

APPOINT AS / APPOINT ..
TO BE / APPOINTS .. TO BE

EXAMPLE

The Grantor appoints a
Person to be Executor.

LEXON 0.2

AT ALL TIMES PROVIDED
general verification condition

at all times provided [that] <binary>

VERIFICATION

This term allows for formal verification, enforcing that certain names may have only certain values under certain conditions. Performance of code stops when a verification fails.

LEXON 0.6

EXAMPLE

At all times provided that the Owner is This Contract or the Escrow is greater or equal to the Minimal Cost.

AT ANY TIME

access control

FILLER

This keyword allows to articulate who should be allowed to initiate the performance of a given clause.

LEXON 0.2

EXAMPLE

CLAUSE: Change.
At any time the Grantor
may fix the Share.

AT LEAST
size of a number

COMPARISON

This is an comparison operator to compare two values. It operates on names and literal values. Comparisons are used to assigned the binary result to names, to inform the performance of the code and to evaluate verification claims.

LEXON 0.3

EXAMPLE

The Initiator sets the "Processing Reward" to any amount that is at least 0.

BE

type definition, assignments and comparisons

"\<name>" be [a] \<type>.
"\<name>" be \<value>.

1. Used to signify that a name will have the meaning of a given type, like a time (type: time) or a number (type: amount).
2. Part of multiple grammar constructs to define or change the meaning of names.

ASSIGNMENT

This term is used to define the value of a name.

SYNONYMS

IS

LEXON 0.2

EXAMPLE

"Grantor" be a person.
"Due Date" be tomorrow.

BE MADE
optional part of a predicate to increase readability

FILLER

This is a filler that is ignored by the Lexon transpiler and virtusal machine. It can be ommitted with no change to script functionality. The legal prose output, however, could be affected.

LEXON 0.6

EXAMPLE

A Status Notification be made.

BEFORE OR ON

earlier in time

COMPARISON

This is an comparison operator to compare two values. It operates on names and literal values. Comparisons are used to assigned the binary result to names, to inform the performance of the code and to evaluate verification claims.

LEXON 0.3

EXAMPLE

The Service Provider may, if Time of Provision of Services is before or on Due Date, and Provision of Services Have Met the Defined Service Criteria then pay the Service Fee from escrow to themselves, and also pay the Fee from escrow to the Assessor.

BEING

same value

COMPARISON

This is an comparison operator to compare two values. It operates on names and literal values. Comparisons are used to assigned the binary result to names, to inform the performance of the code and to evaluate verification claims.

LEXON 0.3

EXAMPLE

CLAUSE: Voting Phase Expired.
"Voting Phase Expired" is defined as the Current Period Number being greater than the Last Voting Phase Period Number.

BEING ON RECORD
optional term to increase readability

FILLER

This is a filler that is ignored by the Lexon transpiler and virtual machine. It can be ommitted with no change to script functionality. The legal prose output, however, could be affected.

LEXON 0.3

EXAMPLE

"Having Never Voted Yes" is defined as no Latest Yes Vote being on record.

BINARY

yes or now / true or false

"<name>" is binary.

TYPE

This is a type name, which is used to clarify what kind of data which name definition might stand for. A type name can be used like a definition, i.e. a name could be defined that has the same name like its type. But no definition may have the name of a type other than its own.

LEXON 0.3

EXAMPLE

"Exceptional Status" is binary.

BURN

delete tokens

burn [the] escrow

burn <number> of <name>

CRYPTO

This term articulates the sending and receipt of crypto currency and any type of token.

LEXON 0.3

EXAMPLE

Burn the remainder of the escrow.

CALCULATE

execute and output result

calculate <formula>

OUTPUT

This is a keyword that signals a result that the performance of the code should share with the world: e.g. print to the screen or write to the blockchain receipt log. Results can often be encrypted to facilitate controlled sharing of private information.

LEXON 0.3

EXAMPLE

CLAUSE: Current Period Number.
The "Current Period Number" is defined as the whole number resulting from calculating the time passed since Summoning Time, divided by the Period Duration.

CERTIFY
optional predicate

FILLER

This is a filler that is ignored by the Lexon transpiler and virtual machine. It can be ommitted with no change to script functionality. The legal prose output, however, could be affected.

EXAMPLE

A Member may certify a Vote.

VARIANTS

BE CERTIFIED

SYNONYMS

SIGN

LEXON 0.2

CLAUSE

start of a clause of the code

CLAUSE: <name>.

CLAUSE starts a subsection of code or an algorithmic definition. It is followed by a name of the subsection or definition. This name can be used to allow state transition of the contract system: in terms of the blockchain implementation of the contract, that a person triggers this clause from a browser interface and with this, initiates the changes to the contact state that the clause might describe. Not all clauses are for this purpose, others are simply groups of statements that are relevant for other clauses or used to facilitate nesting of decisions trees. For example, Lexon really allows for only one if-statement per clause. To nest multiple if-statements, the lower order ones will be subsurmized under their own clause.Good style will use clauses to replace definitons that include calculations.

From the perspective of programming, the CLAUSE keyword serves as a 'function head' and to separate the logic of a script into smaller units, in a fine granulity as used in functional languages.

GRAMMAR

This is a word that is part of the meta structure of Lexon code. It groups and gives meaning to the terms following it.

LEXON 0.2

EXAMPLE

CLAUSE: Set Up.

SYNONYMS

CHAPTER

COLLECT

withdraw tokens

collect <amount> from <person>

CRYPTO

This term articulates the sending and receipt of crypto currency and any type of token.

LEXON 0.3

EXAMPLE

Collect the Proposal Deposit in Approved Tokens from the Proposer to the escrow.

COMMENT
non-processing text

COMMENT: <comment text>

Anything after the COMMENT keyword is ignored for the contract performance until the next line break. Dots are assumed to be part of a comment. The comment can be multiple lines on a printout or on-screen if the program editor or the word editor chose to display text wrapped across multiple lines. The comment still ends only after the place where the enter key had been hit to start a new line.

GRAMMAR

This is a word that is part of the meta structure of Lexon code. It groups and gives meaning to the terms following it.

LEXON 0.1

EXAMPLE

COMMENT: A last will
with multiple recipients

CONSIDER

set binary true

<name> is considered <state>.

ASSIGNMENT

This term is used to define the value of a name.

LEXON 0.3

EXAMPLE

The Proposal is considered Processed.

CONTRACTS

code relating to individual legal agreements

CONTRACTS [as] per <name>:

All code after the CONTRACTS keyword is interpreted to define the 1:1 relationship between two contracting partys. Code part for the 1:1 logic between contract partners, as opposed to the TERMS part that holds statements that are relevant across all individual contracts.

This is mainly an issue of perspective. Definitions under CONTRACTS are per-agreement: they usually exist multiple times eventually, once for every contract.

GRAMMAR

This is a word that is part of the meta structure of Lexon code. It groups and gives meaning to the terms following it.

LEXON 0.2

EXAMPLE

CONTRACTS as per Partner:

COUNT OF

optional indicator that the value and not the name is used for a calculation

FILLER

This is a filler that is ignored by the Lexon transpiler and virtusal machine. It can be ommitted with no change to script functionality. The legal prose output, however, could be affected.

LEXON 0.3

EXAMPLE

Increase the count of No Votes by the number of the Shares of the Member.

CURRENT
optional indicator that a value as recorded at the time is referred to

FILLER

This is a filler that is ignored by the Lexon transpiler and virtusal machine. It can be ommitted with no change to script functionality. The legal prose output, however, could be affected.

LEXON 0.6

EXAMPLE

The "Current Tax" be defined as the product of the current Cost and the current Tax.

CURRENT TIME
point in time

current time

VALUE

This is a value that a name can be defined to have or that the meaning of a name can be compared against. It can also be used to articulate verifications.

LEXON 0.2

EXAMPLE

Data be certified,
with Time fixed as the
current time.

DATA

a hash

"\<name>" is data

This keyword is used to state that a name stands for the unique identifier for a data set, e.g. its cryptographic hash.

TYPE

This is a type name, which is used to clarify what kind of data which name definition might stand for. A type name can be used like a definition, i.e. a name could be defined that has the same name like its type. But no definition may have the name of a type other than its own.

EXAMPLE

"Data" is data.

VARIANTS

DATA FINGERPRINT

SYNONYMS

CRYPTOLOGICAL FINGERPRINT

LEXON 0.2

DATE

a point in time, expressed as a calendar day

"<name>" is [a] date

This keyword is used to state that a name will mean a time, consisting of a date and a time with precision of one second.

TYPE

This is a type name, which is used to clarify what kind of data which name definition might stand for. A type name can be used like a definition, i.e. a name could be defined that has the same name like its type. But no definition may have the name of a type other than its own.

LEXON 0.1

EXAMPLE

"Deadline" is a date.

DAY
time duration

day

UNIT

This is a unit for values, it can also be used to mean 1 unit of this.

LEXON 0.3

EXAMPLE

"Tax Frequency" is a time duration, greater than 1 day.

DECREASE

subtraction

decrease <name> by <value>

<name> are decreased by <value>

MATH

This is an algorithmic operator to calculate results from given values. Its operators can be names and literal values. Such operations are used to calculate values to be assigned to names, to make comparisons that will inform the performance and to evaluate verification claims.

LEXON 0.2

EXAMPLE

Decreased Owned Shares by the Given Amount.

DECREASED BY
subtraction

decrease \<name\> by \<value\>
\<name\> are decreased by \<value\>

MATH

This is an algorithmic operator to calculate results from given values. Its operators can be names and literal values. Such operations are used to calculate values to be assigned to names, to make comparisons that will inform the performance and to evaluate verification claims.

LEXON 0.2

EXAMPLE

The "Last Voting Phase Period Number" be defined as the sum of the Starting Period Number and the Voting Phase Duration In Periods decreased by 1.

DEEM

set binary true

<name> is deemed <state>

ASSIGNMENT

This term is used to define the value of a name.

LEXON 0.2

EXAMPLE

The Proposal is deemed Passed.

DEFINE

assign meaning to a name

"<name>" is defined to be <value>.

Used to define the meaning of a name.

Define works only for names that did not have a meaning assigned before. To change a name's meaning, use 'redefine' or 'change'.

ASSIGNMENT

This term is used to define the value of a name.

VARIANTS

DEFINES / DEFINED / DEFINED TO BE

SYNONYMS

APPOINT, FIX

LEXON 0.2

EXAMPLE

"Due Date" is defined to be Tomorrow.

DIFFERENCE

result of subtraction

difference between <value> and <value>

MATH

This is an algorithmic operator to calculate results from given values. Its operators can be names and literal values. Such operations are used to calculate values to be assigned to names, to make comparisons that will inform the performance and to evaluate verification claims.

LEXON 0.2

EXAMPLE

The Maintainer may: pay the difference between the amount in Escrow and the Minimal Cost from the Escrow to themselves.

DIVIDED BY

mathematical division

<value> devided by <value>

MATH

This is an algorithmic operator to calculate results from given values. Its operators can be names and literal values. Such operations are used to calculate values to be assigned to names, to make comparisons that will inform the performance and to evaluate verification claims.

LEXON 0.2

EXAMPLE

t0 plus t2 to the power of 2 divided by t2.

DIVIDING

mathematical division

dividing \<value\> by \<value\>

MATH

This is an algorithmic operator to calculate results from given values. Its operators can be names and literal values. Such operations are used to calculate values to be assigned to names, to make comparisons that will inform the performance and to evaluate verification claims.

LEXON 0.3

EXAMPLE

The "Voting Phase Periods" is defined as the whole number resulting from dividing the Voting Phase Duration by the Period Duration.

DURATION

a duration of time, precise to the second

"<name>" is [a] duration of time.

This keyword is used to state that a name will mean a duration of time, expressed in years, months, weeks, days, hours, minutes or seconds.

TYPE

This is a type name, which is used to clarify what kind of data which name definition might stand for. A type name can be used like a definition, i.e. a name could be defined that has the same name like its type. But no definition may have the name of a type other than its own.

LEXON 0.2

EXAMPLE

"Period" is defined as a duration of a fifth of a day.

ENTER

create a new legal contract

PERFORMANCE

This term controls the performance of the code, e.g. if following statements apply, or not; or if the contract should terminate.

LEXON 0.3

EXAMPLE

The Summoner enters into a Member Contract with Summoner's Initial Number Of Shares.

ESCROW

the balance of a smart contract, over all individual individual contracts

"<name>" is [an] escrow

This keyword is used to state that a variable contains the special value of the crypto currency balance that is held in the contract.

TYPE

This is a type name, which is used to clarify what kind of data which name definition might stand for. A type name can be used like a definition, i.e. a name could be defined that has the same name like its type. But no definition may have the name of a type other than its own.

EXAMPLE

"Inheritance" is an escrow.

VARIANTS

INTO ESCROW / FROM ESCROW

LEXON 0.2

FIFTH
result of division by five

fifth [of] [a] <value>

MATH

This is an algorithmic operator to calculate results from given values. Its operators can be names and literal values. Such operations are used to calculate values to be assigned to names, to make comparisons that will inform the performance and to evaluate verification claims.

LEXON 0.3

EXAMPLE

"Period Duration" is defined as a duration of a fifth of a day.

FIX

assign meaning to a name

\<person\> fix[es] \<name\>

ASSIGNMENT

This term is used to define the value of a name.

SYNONYMS

SET, APPOINT

EXAMPLE

The Provider fixes the Fee.

LEXON 0.2

FOR ALL

operation across all contracts

for all <name> <clause>

AGGREGATION

This is an aggregation of all values across all contracts of a given type, e.g. summing up individual balances.

LEXON 0.2

EXAMPLE

CLAUSE: Execute.
The Executor may
for all Heirs Payout.

FOURTH
result of division by four

fourth [of] [a] <value>

MATH

This is an algorithmic operator to calculate results from given values. Its operators can be names and literal values. Such operations are used to calculate values to be assigned to names, to make comparisons that will inform the performance and to evaluate verification claims.

LEXON 0.3

EXAMPLE

"Period Duration" is defined as a duration of a fourth of a day.

FURTHER IN THE FUTURE THAN

later in time

further in the future than <duration of time>

COMPARISON

This is an comparison operator to compare two values. It operates on names and literal values. Comparisons are used to assigned the binary result to names, to inform the performance of the code and to evaluate verification claims.

LEXON 0.6

EXAMPLE

At all times provided that Next Tax Due Date is not further in the future than the number of days given as Tax Frequency.

GIVEN

optional indicator that a value as recorded at the time is referred to

FILLER

This is a filler that is ignored by the Lexon transpiler and virtusal machine. It can be ommitted with no change to script functionality. The legal prose output, however, could be affected.

LEXON 0.6

EXAMPLE

At all times provided that Next Tax Due Date is not further in the future than the number of days given as Tax Frequency.

GREATER OR EQUAL TO
compare two values

greater or equal [to] <value>

COMPARISON

This is an comparison operator to compare two values. It operates on names and literal values. Comparisons are used to assigned the binary result to names, to inform the performance of the code and to evaluate verification claims.

LEXON 0.1

EXAMPLE

"Cost" is an amount, greater or equal to 0.

GREATER THAN
compare two values

greater than <value>

COMPARISON

This is an comparison operator to compare two values. It operates on names and literal values. Comparisons are used to assigned the binary result to names, to inform the performance of the code and to evaluate verification claims.

LEXON 0.1

EXAMPLE

"Cost" is an amount, greater than 0.

HALF
result of division by two

half [of] [a] <value>

MATH

This is an algorithmic operator to calculate results from given values. Its operators can be names and literal values. Such operations are used to calculate values to be assigned to names, to make comparisons that will inform the performance and to evaluate verification claims.

LEXON 0.3

EXAMPLE

"Period Duration" is defined as a duration of a half day.

HAVING BEEN
binary being true

having been <binary>

COMPARISON

This is an comparison operator to compare two values. It operates on names and literal values. Comparisons are used to assigned the binary result to names, to inform the performance of the code and to evaluate verification claims.

LEXON 0.3

EXAMPLE

Eligibility To Ragequit is defined as Having Never Voted Yes
or the Proposal of the Latest Yes Vote having been Processed.

IF ... THEN: ... ELSE:

optional code branches

PERFORMANCE

This term controls the performance of the code, e.g. if following statements apply, or not; or if the contract should terminate.

LEXON 0.2

EXAMPLE

If the Possessor is not the Owner,
then: Hand Over to the Exception Handler;
else: Set Next Tax Date,
afterwards Update Records,
and afterwards publish Owner and Cost.

IN

diverse uses as filler and part of other key word terms

MULTIPLE MEANINGS

The word "in" is part of other keywords / key terms.

LEXON 0.2

EXAMPLE

If in Exceptional Status,
the Exception Handler
may:
redefine the Possessor to
be any person.

An Applicant may offer a
Token Tribute in
Approved Tokens, set
the Shares Requested,
set the Details,
and by this Create a
Proposal with the Shares
Requested.

IN ANY CASE

optional reaffirmation that all sentences in a clause are independent declarations

FILLER

This is a filler that is ignored by the Lexon transpiler and virtusal machine. It can be ommitted with no change to script functionality. The legal prose output, however, could be affected.

LEXON 0.2

EXAMPLE

In any case, afterwards terminate this contract.

INCREASE
mathematical addition

increase \<name\> by \<value\>

MATH

This is an algorithmic operator to calculate results from given values. Its operators can be names and literal values. Such operations are used to calculate values to be assigned to names, to make comparisons that will inform the performance and to evaluate verification claims.

LEXON 0.2

EXAMPLE

The Total Shares Requested are increased by the Shares Requested.

Increase the count of No Votes by the number of the Shares of the Member.

INCREASED BY

mathematical addition

<value> increased by <value>

MATH

This is an algorithmic operator to calculate results from given values. Its operators can be names and literal values. Such operations are used to calculate values to be assigned to names, to make comparisons that will inform the performance and to evaluate verification claims.

LEXON 0.2

EXAMPLE

The Starting Period Number be defined as the Last Blocked Period Number increased by 1.

INVOKE

set binary true

<binary> be invoked.

ASSIGNMENT

This term is used to define the value of a name.

VARIANTS

BE ... INVOKED

LEXON 0.3

EXAMPLE

Exceptional Status be invoked.

IS

type definitions, assignments and comparisons

"<name>" is [a] <type>.
If <definition> is <value>, then:
<statements>.
"<name>" is redefined to be <value>.

1. Used to signify that a variable will have the content of a given type, like a time (type: time) or a number (type: amount).
2. Part of multiple grammar constructs to redefine definitions or make comparisons.
3. Test of existance in a specific list, i.e. having certain attributes.

ASSIGNMENT / COMPARISON

This is an comparison operator to compare two values. It operates on names and literal values. Comparisons are used to assigned the binary result to names, to inform the performance of the code and to evaluate verification claims. / This term is used to define the value of a name.

EXAMPLE

"Due Date" is redefined to be tomorrow.

If the Applicant is not a Member then, Enlist Applicant as Member.

LEXON 0.2

LESS OR EQUAL TO
compare two values

less or equal [to] <value>

COMPARISON

This is an comparison operator to compare two values. It operates on names and literal values. Comparisons are used to assigned the binary result to names, to inform the performance of the code and to evaluate verification claims.

LEXON 0.1

EXAMPLE

"Cost" is an amount, less or equal to 100.

LESS THAN

compare two values

less than <duration of time>

COMPARISON

This is an comparison operator to compare two values. It operates on names and literal values. Comparisons are used to assigned the binary result to names, to inform the performance of the code and to evaluate verification claims.

LEXON 0.1

EXAMPLE

"Cost" is an amount, less than 100.

LEX

start of lexon code

LEX <name>.

LEX is the keyword that starts the Lexon script. It is mandatory and it is immediately followed by the name for the smart contract (or contract system consisting of multiple contracts) that is being defined. After the name, a dot is expected. Definitions, and CLAUSES will usually follow below, often divided in a TERMS and CONTRACTS section.

GRAMMAR

This is a word that is part of the meta structure of Lexon code. It groups and gives meaning to the terms following it.

LEXON 0.2

EXAMPLE

LEX Will.

LEXON

script version follows

LEXON: <version>

This optional tag helps to stay oriented about the different versions of Lexon that code and code examples are made for. E.g. an example for Lexon 0.2 might not work for 0.3 and actually be misleading. This is aspect is important enough in practice that it warrants its own keyword. In general, older code will often not run with newer versions of the compiler, as is normal for programming languages. The expectation is that code within one 'minor' version number (e.g. the 2 in 0.2.0) will be compatible: i.e. code for 0.2.0 should run with Lexon 0.2.1 but NOT vice versa. This is only a rule of thumb though and the cost of staying always true to this convention might sometimes be forbidding. After Lexon 1.0, no compatibility breaking changes are expected until Lexon 2.0. The version number can currently be completely free form, it is not automatically processed yet but only an indication to users.

GRAMMAR

This is a word that is part of the meta structure of Lexon code. It groups and gives meaning to the terms following it.

LEXON 0.2

EXAMPLE

LEXON: 0.2.9

MAKE A PAYMENT
send tokens

\<person\> makes a payment [to escrow]
\<comparison\>

CRYPTO

This term articulates the sending and receipt of crypto currency and any type of token.

VARIANTS

MAKES A PAYMENT

LEXON 0.6

EXAMPLE

If the Owner makes a Payment to Escrow equal to the Current Tax, then the Next Tax Due Date is redefined to be the time of Tax Frequency later than it was before.

MAY

permission to specific acting person

`<person> may <statement>`

Only the person named before 'may' can initiate the performance of what is described in a clause. No one can initiate the performance of a clause that is not lead in with a 'may', except by reference from another clause. This is the main organizational element to assign rights in a contract.

PERMISSION

This keyword allows to articulate who should be allowed to initiate the performance of a given clause.

LEXON 0.1

EXAMPLE

The Executor may pay the Inheritance to the Heir.

MINUS

subtract

<value> minus <value>

MATH

This is an algorithmic operator to calculate results from given values. Its operators can be names and literal values. Such operations are used to calculate values to be assigned to names, to make comparisons that will inform the performance and to evaluate verification claims.

LEXON 0.2

EXAMPLE

The "Last Voting Phase Period Number" be defined as the sum of the Starting Period Number and the Voting Phase Duration In Periods minus 1.

MUST

verification condition

<name> must [be] <value>

VERIFICATION

This term allows for formal verification, enforcing that certain names may have only certain values under certain conditions. Performance of code stops when a verification fails.

LEXON 0.3

EXAMPLE

The Vote must be "yes" or "no".

NEVER

disallow a value

never <value>

never <type>

VERIFICATION

This term allows for formal verification, enforcing that certain names may have only certain values under certain conditions. Performance of code stops when a verification fails.

LEXON 0.6

EXAMPLE

"Owner" is a person, and never no one.

NO
binary

no

VALUE

This is a value that a name can be defined to have or that the meaning of a name can be compared against. It can also be used to articulate verifications.

LEXON 0.3

EXAMPLE

The Vote must be "yes" or "no".

NO-ONE

enforce a person to be appointed

no-one

VALUE

This is a value that a name can be defined to have or that the meaning of a name can be compared against. It can also be used to articulate verifications.

LEXON 0.6

EXAMPLE

"Owner" is a person, and never no one.

NOT

inverse binary

not \<binary>

COMPARISON

This is an comparison operator to compare two values. It operates on names and literal values. Comparisons are used to assigned the binary result to names, to inform the performance of the code and to evaluate verification claims.

LEXON 0.2

EXAMPLE

Also provided that the Owner is not This Contract.

NOT THE CASE

comparison of binary to true

not the case [that] <binary>

TEST

This is an comparison operator that operates on a binary value. It operates on names and literal values. Comparisons are used to assigned the binary result to names, to inform the performance of the code and to evaluate verification claims.

LEXON 0.3

EXAMPLE

CHAPTER: Pay Back.
The Client may if Due Date is past and it is not the case that Provision of Services Have Met the Defined Service Criteria pay the Service Fee from escrow to themselves, and also pay the Fee from escrow to the Assessor.

NOTIFY

record a result

notify <person>

<person> be notified.

OUTPUT

This is a keyword that signals a result that the performance of the code should share with the world: e.g. print to the screen or write to the blockchain receipt log. Results can often be encrypted to facilitate controlled sharing of private information.

EXAMPLE

The Exception Handler be notified.

VARIANTS

BE ... NOTIFIED

SYNONYMS

SEND A NOTIFICATION

LEXON 0.3

NOW

point in time

now

VALUE

This is a value that a name can be defined to have or that the meaning of a name can be compared against. It can also be used to articulate verifications.

LEXON 0.2

EXAMPLE

Next Tax Due Date be redefined as the time given in Tax Frequency after now.

NUMBER OF

optional indicator that the value and not the name is used for a calculation

FILLER

This is a filler that is ignored by the Lexon transpiler and virtusal machine. It can be ommitted with no change to script functionality. The legal prose output, however, could be affected.

LEXON 0.3

EXAMPLE

increase the count of No Votes by the number of the Shares of the Member.

NUMBER OF DAYS

optional indicator that the value and not the name is used for a calculation

FILLER

This is a filler that is ignored by the Lexon transpiler and virtusal machine. It can be ommitted with no change to script functionality. The legal prose output, however, could be affected.

LEXON 0.6

EXAMPLE

At all times provided that Next Tax Due Date is not further in the future than the number of days given as Tax Frequency.

OFFER

send tokens

<person> [may] offer[s] [a] <amount>

CRYPTO

This term articulates the sending and receipt of crypto currency and any type of token.

LEXON 0.3

EXAMPLE

An Applicant may offer a Token Tribute in Approved Tokens, set the Shares Requested, set the Details, and by this Create a Proposal with the Shares Requested.

ON

comparison of binary to true

<binary> on

TEST

This is an comparison operator that operates on a binary value. It operates on names and literal values. Comparisons are used to assigned the binary result to names, to inform the performance of the code and to evaluate verification claims.

LEXON 0.3

EXAMPLE

Provided there is no Exceptional Status on.

OR

options

<binary> or <binary>

<type> or <type>

COMPARISON

This is an comparison operator to compare two values. It operates on names and literal values. Comparisons are used to assigned the binary result to names, to inform the performance of the code and to evaluate verification claims.

LEXON 0.1

EXAMPLE

"Possessor" is a person, or no one.

PAID

optional reaffirmation that an amount has been paid in prior

FILLER

This is a filler that is ignored by the Lexon transpiler and virtusal machine. It can be ommitted with no change to script functionality. The legal prose output, however, could be affected.

LEXON 0.6

EXAMPLE

Refund the paid Amount from Escrow to the Purchaser.

PASSED

earlier in time

\<point in time\> [has] passed

COMPARISON

This is an comparison operator to compare two values. It operates on names and literal values. Comparisons are used to assigned the binary result to names, to inform the performance of the code and to evaluate verification claims.

VARIANTS

HAS PASSED

LEXON 0.2

EXAMPLE

Anyone may: if Next Tax Due Date has passed, then: Trigger The Default.

PAST

earlier in time

<point in time> [is] past

COMPARISON

This is an comparison operator to compare two values. It operates on names and literal values. Comparisons are used to assigned the binary result to names, to inform the performance of the code and to evaluate verification claims.

LEXON 0.2

EXAMPLE

If Time for Next Payment is now or past then pay an Installment to themselves, and afterwards if the escrow is 0 then terminate this contract else increase the Time for Next Payment by the Time between Payments.

PAY .. TO

send tokens

<person> pays <amount> to <person>.

Send or receive crypto currency, depending on the receiver. 'Escrow' is the described smart contract system itself.

CRYPTO

This term articulates the sending and receipt of crypto currency and any type of token.

EXAMPLE

The Grantor pays an Inheritance into Escrow.

VARIANTS

PAYS .. TO / PAYS IN / PAYS .. INTO ESCROW / IS PAID INTO ESCROW

SYNONYMS

SEND, RETURN

LEXON 0.2

PERSON

a blockchain account or address

"<name>" is a person.

TYPE

This is a type name, which is used to clarify what kind of data which name definition might stand for. A type name can be used like a definition, i.e. a name could be defined that has the same name like its type. But no definition may have the name of a type other than its own.

LEXON 0.1

EXAMPLE

"Grantor" is a person.

PLUS

add

<value> plus <value>

MATH

This is an algorithmic operator to calculate results from given values. Its operators can be names and literal values. Such operations are used to calculate values to be assigned to names, to make comparisons that will inform the performance and to evaluate verification claims.

LEXON 0.2

EXAMPLE

t0 plus t2 to the power of 2 divided by t2.

POWER OF

mathemical exponent

<value> to [the] power of <value>

MATH

This is an algorithmic operator to calculate results from given values. Its operators can be names and literal values. Such operations are used to calculate values to be assigned to names, to make comparisons that will inform the performance and to evaluate verification claims.

LEXON 0.2

EXAMPLE

t0 plus t2 to the power of 2 divided by t2.

PREVIOUS

prior value of a name

previous <name>

REFLECTION

This keyword allows to reach back to previous definitions of a name.

LEXON 0.6

EXAMPLE

Increase the count of Cases by the amount of previous Attempts.

PRIOR

prior value of a name

prior <name>

REFLECTION

This keyword allows to reach back to previous definitions of a name.

LEXON 0.6

EXAMPLE

Decrease the number of Tokens by the prior balance.

PRODUCT OF ... AND

result of multiplication

product of <value> and <value>

MATH

This is an algorithmic operator to calculate results from given values. Its operators can be names and literal values. Such operations are used to calculate values to be assigned to names, to make comparisons that will inform the performance and to evaluate verification claims.

LEXON 0.3

EXAMPLE

The "Cost" be redefined as the product of the former Cost and the EPS.

PROVIDED

start of a verification condition of a clause

provided <binary>

VERIFICATION

This term allows for formal verification, enforcing that certain names may have only certain values under certain conditions. Performance of code stops when a verification fails.

LEXON 0.3

EXAMPLE

Provided there is no Exceptional Status on.

PUBLISH

record a result

publish <name>

OUTPUT

This is a keyword that signals a result that the performance of the code should share with the world: e.g. print to the screen or write to the blockchain receipt log. Results can often be encrypted to facilitate controlled sharing of private information.

LEXON 0.3

EXAMPLE

Set Next Tax Date, afterwards Update Records, and afterwards publish Owner and Cost.

RECORD

optional reaffirmation that the invocation of a clause will change the state of a contract

FILLER

This is a filler that is ignored by the Lexon transpiler and virtusal machine. It can be ommitted with no change to script functionality. The legal prose output, however, could be affected.

LEXON 0.3

EXAMPLE

Increase the count of Yes Votes by the number of the Shares of the Member,
and also record the Last Vote of the Member,
and also Track Maximum of Total Yes Votes.

RECORDED VALUE

optional indicator that the current value of a definition is used for a calculation

FILLER

This is a filler that is ignored by the Lexon transpiler and virtusal machine. It can be ommitted with no change to script functionality. The legal prose output, however, could be affected.

LEXON 0.3

EXAMPLE

If the count of Total Shares is greater than the recorded value of Maximum Total Shares At Yes Vote then the recorded value of Maximum Total Shares At Yes Vote be changed at that point to the count of Total Shares.

REDEFINE

change the meaning of a name

"<name>" is redefined to be <value>.

Used to change the meaning of a name.

Define works only for names that did not have a meaning assigned before. To change a name's meaning, use 'redefine' or 'change'.

Good style avoids redefinitions as they can degrade readability of code.

ASSIGNMENT

This term is used to define the value of a name.

VARIANTS

REDEFINES / REDEFINED / REDEFINED TO BE

SYNONYMS

CHANGE

EXAMPLE

"Due Date" is redefined to be Tomorrow.

LEXON 0.2

REMAINDER
remainder of division or escrow

remainder of the escrow

remainder of <division>

1. Remainder of a division of whole numbers.
2. Remainder of the amount in escrow.

MATH / CRYPTO

This is an algorithmic operator to calculate results from given values. Its operators can be names and literal values. Such operations are used to calculate values to be assigned to names, to make comparisons that will inform the performance and to evaluate verification claims. / This term articulates the sending and receipt of crypto currency and any type of token.

LEXON 0.2

EXAMPLE

Return the remainder of the escrow to the Payer.

RESULTING

optional filler indicating that a name is re-defined by a calculation

FILLER

This is a filler that is ignored by the Lexon transpiler and virtual machine. It can be ommitted with no change to script functionality. The legal prose output, however, could be affected.

LEXON 0.3

EXAMPLE

The "Voting Phase Periods" is defined as the whole number resulting from dividing the Voting Phase Duration by the Period Duration.

RETURN

send tokens back

return <amount> to <person>

Send received crypto currency back to the sender.

CRYPTO

This term articulates the sending and receipt of crypto currency and any type of token.

EXAMPLE

Return the Payment to the Customer.

SYNONYMS

PAY

LEXON 0.2

REVEAL

record a result

reveal <value> to <person>

OUTPUT

This is a keyword that signals a result that the performance of the code should share with the world: e.g. print to the screen or write to the blockchain receipt log. Results can often be encrypted to facilitate controlled sharing of private information.

LEXON 0.2

EXAMPLE

The Owner may reveal Data and Time to a Viewer.

REVOKE

set binary false

revoke <binary>

ASSIGNMENT

This term is used to define the value of a name.

LEXON 0.2

EXAMPLE

CLAUSE: End
Exceptional Status.
If in Exceptional Status,
the Exception Handler
may:
revoke the Exceptional
Status.

SECONDS

time duration

seconds

UNIT

This is a unit for values, it can also be used to mean 1 unit of this.

LEXON 0.3

EXAMPLE

The "Period Duration" is set to a duration of time in seconds, greater than 0.

SECTION

non-processing headline

SECTION: <headline text>

A headline comment that has no meaning for the program execution and is ignored. It is used to signify a logical part in the code without having any binding meaning for the performance. It can be used entirely freely to improve readability for humans. Anything after the SECTION keyword is ignored for the contract performance until the next line break. Dots are assumed to be part of a comment. The section headline text can be multiple lines on a printout or on-screen if the program editor or the word editor chose to display text wrapped across multiple lines. The section headline text still ends only after the place where the enter key had been hit to start a new line.

GRAMMAR

This is a reserved keyword that has significant meaning to the Lexon transpiler and virtual machine. It cannot be used as a variable or contract name. It does not matter whether any of its letters are written in lower or upper case. But other words can include this keyword as part.

LEXON 0.2

EXAMPLE

SECTION: TAX.

SEND A NOTIFICATION
record a result

send a notification to <person> to
<message>

OUTPUT

This is a keyword that signals a result that the performance of the code should share with the world: e.g. print to the screen or write to the blockchain receipt log. Results can often be encrypted to facilitate controlled sharing of private information.

EXAMPLE

Afterwards, send a
Notification that a
Default occurred,
and send a Notification
to the Possessor to send
the Notebook to the
Owner.

SYNONYMS

NOTIFY

LEXON 0.6

SUBTRACT FROM
subtraction

subtract \<value\> from \<value\>

MATH

This is an algorithmic operator to calculate results from given values. Its operators can be names and literal values. Such operations are used to calculate values to be assigned to names, to make comparisons that will inform the performance and to evaluate verification claims.

LEXON 0.2

EXAMPLE

subtract test var1 from test var2.

SUM OF
result of addition

sum of [all] <name> <contractor>

MATH

This is an algorithmic operator to calculate results from given values. Its operators can be names and literal values. Such operations are used to calculate values to be assigned to names, to make comparisons that will inform the performance and to evaluate verification claims.

LEXON 0.2

EXAMPLE

CLAUSE: Payout.
Pay the Inheritance times
the Share
divided by the sum of all
Shares to the Heir,
and thereby terminate
this contract.

TENTH

result of division by ten

tenth [of] [a] <value>

MATH

This is an algorithmic operator to calculate results from given values. Its operators can be names and literal values. Such operations are used to calculate values to be assigned to names, to make comparisons that will inform the performance and to evaluate verification claims.

LEXON 0.3

EXAMPLE

"Wait" is defined as a duration of a tenth of a day.

TERMINATE
end the performance

\<person\> may terminate this contract.

No contract clause can be performed after this statement has been met. The original creator can access any remaining balance.

PERFORMANCE

This term controls the performance of the code, e.g. if following statements apply, or not; or if the contract should terminate.

LEXON 0.2

EXAMPLE

The Executor may pay the Escrow to the Heir and thereby Terminate this contract.

TERMINATE ALL CONTRACTS.

partly end performance

PERFORMANCE

This term controls the performance of the code, e.g. if following statements apply, or not; or if the contract should terminate.

LEXON 0.2

EXAMPLE

The Executor may
for all Heirs Payout,
and thereby terminate all
contracts.

TERMS

start of the optional code section that contains statements that are relevant across multiple contracts.

TERMS:

Code after TERMS and until the CONTRACTS keyword appears, is understood to be relevant across many different contracts. Those contracts are then defined under the CONTRACTS section.

The code after TERMS will usually start with definitions, followed by preparatory instructions and then clauses. All of this is optional and the TERMS keyword can be left out when there is no CONTACTS keyword below.

GRAMMAR

This is a word that is part of the meta structure of Lexon code. It groups and gives meaning to the terms following it.

LEXON 0.2

EXAMPLE

TERMS:

TEXT

a value that containts a word, a text, letters or numbers

"<name>" is [a] text.

This type is used to state that a variable will contain a blockchain address, or a blockchain account, which is the way that ids exist on a blockchain.

TYPE

This is a type name, which is used to clarify what kind of data which name definition might stand for. A type name can be used like a definition, i.e. a name could be defined that has the same name like its type. But no definition may have the name of a type other than its own.

LEXON 0.2

EXAMPLE

The "Text" is a text.

THE
optional article to increase readability

(none)

FILLER

This is a filler that is ignored by the Lexon transpiler and virtusal machine. It can be ommitted with no change to script functionality. The legal prose output, however, could be affected.

EXAMPLE

The Executor may pay the Escrow to the Heir

SYNONYMS

A, AN

LEXON 0.1

THEMSELVES

pronoun

<person> pay <amount> to themselves.

A pronoun that means the subject of the statement, a person.

PRONOUN

This is a reserved keyword that has significant meaning to the Lexon transpiler and virtual machine. It cannot be used as a variable or contract name. It does not matter whether any of its letters are written in lower or upper case. But other words can include this keyword as part.

LEXON 0.2

EXAMPLE

The Arbiter may pay from escrow the Fee to themselves.

THEN
conditional and chronological order

<statement>, [and] then <statement>

SEQUENCE

This word puts statements before and after it in chronological order. This is a reserved keyword that has significant meaning to the Lexon transpiler and virtual machine. It cannot be used as a variable or contract name. It does not matter whether any of its letters are written in lower or upper case. Other words can include this keyword as part.

LEXON 0.2

EXAMPLE

The Holder may pay the Amount into escrow, and then the Bet is deemed Closed.

THERE IS

optional wording to increase readability of conditions

there is <condition>

FILLER

This is a filler that is ignored by the Lexon transpiler and virtual machine. It can be ommitted with no change to script functionality. The legal prose output, however, could be affected.

LEXON 0.6

EXAMPLE

Provided there is no Exceptional Status on.

THEREBY

conditional and chronological order

<statement> thereby <statement>

indicates that the following statement should come into effect if the preceding was performed. If the preceding statement could not be performed, the following statement should not even be looked at.

SEQUENCE

This word puts statements before and after it in chronological order. This is a reserved keyword that has significant meaning to the Lexon transpiler and virtual machine. It cannot be used as a variable or contract name. It does not matter whether any of its letters are written in lower or upper case. Other words can include this keyword as part.

EXAMPLE

The Executor may pay the Escrow to the Heir and thereby terminate this contract.

VARIANTS

AND THEREBY

SYNONYMS

AFTERWARDS, AND ALSO

LEXON 0.2

THIRD
result of division by three

third [of] [a] <value>

MATH

This is an algorithmic operator to calculate results from given values. Its operators can be names and literal values. Such operations are used to calculate values to be assigned to names, to make comparisons that will inform the performance and to evaluate verification claims.

LEXON 0.3

EXAMPLE

"Cool Down" is defined as a duration of a third of a day.

THIS

optional demonstrative determiner to increase readability

(none)

FILLER

This is a filler that is ignored by the Lexon transpiler and virtual machine. It can be ommitted with no change to script functionality. The legal prose output, however, could be affected.

LEXON 0.3

EXAMPLE

Terminate this Will.

THIS CONTRACT

the address of this code when instantiated on the blockchain

this contract

This definition is always available and stands in for the blockchain identity of the code itself that it is part of. It can be used to define a name that when used makes the code more readable.

VALUE

This is a reserved term that has significant meaning to the Lexon transpiler and virtual machine. It cannot be used as a definition or contract name. It does not matter whether any of its letters are written in lower or upper case. Other words can include this term as part.

EXAMPLE

"Will" is defined as this contract.

LEXON 0.2

TIME
a date and time to the second

"<name>" is [a] time.

This keyword is used to state that a name means a timestamp, consisting of a date and a time with precision of one second.

TYPE

This is a type name, which is used to clarify what kind of data which name definition might stand for. A type name can be used like a definition, i.e. a name could be defined that has the same name like its type. But no definition may have the name of a type other than its own.

LEXON 0.1

EXAMPLE

"Deadline" is a time.

TIME PASSED SINCE

the time span between now and a given time

time passed since <point in time>

MATH

This is an algorithmic operator to calculate results from given values. Its operators can be names and literal values. Such operations are used to calculate values to be assigned to names, to make comparisons that will inform the performance and to evaluate verification claims.

LEXON 0.3

EXAMPLE

CLAUSE: Current Period Number.
The "Current Period Number" is defined as the whole number resulting from calculating the time passed since Summoning Time, divided by the Period Duration.

TIMES

multiplication

<name> times <number>

MATH

This is an algorithmic operator to calculate results from given values. Its operators can be names and literal values. Such operations are used to calculate values to be assigned to names, to make comparisons that will inform the performance and to evaluate verification claims.

LEXON 0.3

EXAMPLE

CLAUSE: Compensation.
Rage Compensation is defined as
the amount in escrow times the Burned Shares divided by the sum of the Total Shares and the Burned Shares.

TO

optional preposition to increase readability

(none)

FILLER

This is a filler that is ignored by the Lexon transpiler and virtusal machine. It can be ommitted with no change to script functionality. The legal prose output, however, could be affected.

LEXON 0.1

EXAMPLE

The Grantor appoints a Person to be Executor.

TOKEN TYPE

the name of the currency or token to be used

TYPE

This is a type name, which is used to clarify what kind of data which name definition might stand for. A type name can be used like a definition, i.e. a name could be defined that has the same name like its type. But no definition may have the name of a type other than its own.

LEXON 0.3

EXAMPLE

The Summoner sets the "Approved Token" to any token type.

TRANSFER

send tokens

<transfer> <amount> [from escrow] to <person>

CRYPTO

This term articulates the sending and receipt of crypto currency and any type of token.

LEXON 0.3

EXAMPLE

Transfer the Token Tribute in Approved Tokens from escrow to Guild Bank.

UNDEFINED
value for 'no value'

undefined

VALUE

This is a value that a name can be defined to have or that the meaning of a name can be compared against. It can also be used to articulate verifications.

LEXON 0.6

EXAMPLE

"Last Status Claimed" is a text, or undefined.

WHOLE NUMBER
discarding decimal fractions of a number

whole number [resulting from]
<formula>

MATH

This is an algorithmic operator to calculate results from given values. Its operators can be names and literal values. Such operations are used to calculate values to be assigned to names, to make comparisons that will inform the performance and to evaluate verification claims.

LEXON 0.3

EXAMPLE

The "Voting Phase Periods" is defined as the whole number resulting from dividing the Voting Phase Duration by the Period Duration.

WITH

list values for a clause

<clause> with <name>

ASSIGNMENT

This term is used to define the value of a name.

LEXON 0.2

EXAMPLE

The Summoner enters into a Member Contract with Summoner's Initial Number Of Shares.

YES

binary true

yes

VALUE

This is a value that a name can be defined to have or that the meaning of a name can be compared against. It can also be used to articulate verifications.

LEXON 0.3

EXAMPLE

The Vote must be "yes" or "no".

APPENDIX

APPENDIX I:
RESOURCES

Please get in touch, break things, let us know.

Feedback   lexon.book@gmail.com

Updates of this list www.lexon.tech/resources

Web Site   www.lexon.tech

Tutorial   www.lexon.tech/tutorial

Docs & Reference   www.lexon.tech/docs

Mailing List   list.lexon.tech

Book   amazon.com/dp/169774768X

                                 ISBN 978-1697747683

Bible   amazon.com/dp/1656262665

                                 ISBN 978-1656262660

Online Editor   demo.lexon.tech

Aeternity Editor   fire.lexon.tech   (lexon-enabled)

Ethereum Editor   remix.ethereum.org   (lexon-enabled)

Lexon Compiler   gitlab.com/lexon-foundation/lexon-rust

WASM Build   npmjs.com/package/lexon-wasm

APPENDIX II:
BLOCKCHAINS
& SMART
CONTRACTS

If you would like to read about the very basic of blockchains, this is for you. Lexon is not only for blockchain and this information is not required knowledge to understand this book.

Blockchains bring a new dimension to information technology: data that cannot be forged, and therefore, can be trusted.[119] Smart contracts are simply programs that process exclusively this trustable data and accordingly, their results can likewise be fully trusted. That they were called 'smart contracts' was not initially meant in the legal sense. But because they can transfer cryptocurrency, they were found to look quite like a sequence of steps to be followed to eventually have money flowing: in other words, much like a contract.

Every single piece of information on a blockchain is signed by who put it into the system. And similar to how a human community works – as a network of individual brains – every participating computer in a blockchain has a copy of

---

[119] Ironically dubbed 'trust-less' by the full-on nerd logic that the data can be relied upon – thanks to cryptography – without having to trust anyone.

everything in the chain. It can therefore independently verify any claim anyone might make about the chain's data. And that's all really.

This is quite an <u>in</u>efficient way to store and process data, the most inefficient way thinkable actually. It also suffers from the *trash-in trash-out* problem: if someone signs a lie, well the lie is in the system. But because of the signature there can be consequences. At least in a blockchain, there are no anonymous lies. This makes for a huge difference.

Because data in a blockchain can also *not* be duplicated – everyone else would notice it immediately because everyone holds full copies – blockchains can support digital cash. Before the advent of Bitcoin this was thought to be impossible. It seemed that everything digital could always be copied. But if everyone has a complete copy, you can't just print yourself more digital coins without the others noticing. That is, you could but *consensus* means that everyone else would simply stop talking to you. No one would take your fake money. Or even your real coins anymore for that matter.

This is how programs in the blockchain – smart contracts – can send money around. Directly, without needing to call Pay-Pal or your bank for it. Because all of a sudden, copy-proofed bits and bytes can be used as cash. This is pretty magical. It can and is used in business and works fast and flawlessly. The reason you might not be hearing much about it is that no-one really earns much from this. It's the basic blockchain functionality.

But it's a game-changing, new super power for programs. Computational Law was not originally concerned with it because no-one saw this coming. The vision that law and contracts should be computable long pre-dated blockchains. But everyone is sure looking to Computational Law now to give context and help to understand what smart contracts are.

Blockchains are the result of 30 years of research originating with the Cypherpunk movement in the 1980s. A movement that was about open rebellion against some laws, utilizing the 'weapon' of writing code. A main motivation to invent the blockchain was concern about the coming surveillance capitalism that we see in full bloom now. The Cypherpunks understood early that what was needed was a decentralized – and ideally private – way to transact. Because the centralized nature of prevailing system architectures is what makes surveillance so cheap.

David Chaum started to write about it in the year 1984, blockchains took it to the next level 25 years later. Bitcoin of course became an Eldorado of knights of fortune and speculators, and the ICO craze of 2017 saw untold pyramid schemes bagging millions. But the original spirit of the movement is captured in this 1993 declaration:

A Cypherpunk's Manifesto

Privacy is necessary for an open society in the electronic age. Privacy is not secrecy. A private matter is something one doesn't want the whole world to know, but a secret matter is something one doesn't want anybody to know. Privacy is the power to selectively reveal oneself to the world.

If two parties have some sort of dealings, then each has a memory of their interaction. Each party can speak about their own memory of this; how could anyone prevent it? One could pass laws against it, but the freedom of speech, even more than privacy, is fundamental to an open society; we seek not to restrict any speech at all. If many parties speak together in the same forum, each can speak to all the others and aggregate together knowledge about individuals and other parties. The power of electronic communications has enabled such group speech, and it will not go away merely because we might want it to.

Since we desire privacy, we must ensure that each party to a transaction have knowledge only of that which is directly necessary for that transaction. Since any information can be spoken of, we must ensure that we reveal as little as possible. In most cases personal identity is not salient. When I purchase a magazine at a store and hand cash to the clerk, there is no need to know who I am. When I ask my electronic mail provider to send and receive messages, my provider need not know to whom I am speaking or what I am saying or what others are saying to me; my provider only need know how to get the message there and how much I owe them in fees. When my identity is revealed by the underlying mechanism of the transaction, I have no privacy. I cannot here selectively reveal myself; I must always reveal myself.

Therefore, privacy in an open society requires anonymous transaction systems. Until now, cash has been the primary such system. An anonymous transaction system is not a secret transaction system. An anonymous system empowers individuals to reveal their identity when desired and only when desired; this is the essence of privacy.

Privacy in an open society also requires cryptography. If I say something, I want it heard only by those for whom I intend it. If the content of my speech is available to the world, I have no privacy. To encrypt is to indicate the desire for privacy, and to encrypt with weak cryptography is to indicate not too much desire for privacy. Furthermore, to reveal one's identity with assurance when the default is anonymity requires the cryptographic signature.

We cannot expect governments, corporations, or other large, faceless organizations to grant us privacy out of their beneficence. It is to their advantage to speak of us, and we should expect that they will speak.. To try to prevent their speech is to fight against the realities of information. Information does not just want to be free, it longs to be free. Information expands to fill the available storage space. Information is Rumor's younger, stronger cousin; Information is fleeter of foot, has more eyes, knows more, and understands less than Rumor.

We must defend our own privacy if we expect to have any. We must come together and create systems which allow anonymous transactions to take place. People have been defending their own privacy for centuries with whispers, darkness, envelopes, closed doors, secret handshakes, and couriers. The technologies of the past did not allow for strong privacy, but electronic technologies do.

We the Cypherpunks are dedicated to building anonymous systems. We are defending our privacy with cryptography, with anonymous mail forwarding systems, with digital signatures, and with electronic money.

Cypherpunks write code. We know that someone has to write software to defend privacy, and since we can't get privacy unless we all do, we're going to write it. We publish our code so that our fellow Cypherpunks may practice and play with it. Our code is free for all to use, worldwide. We don't much care if you don't approve of the software we write. We know that software can't be destroyed and that a widely dispersed system can't be shut down.

Cypherpunks deplore regulations on cryptography, for encryption is fundamentally a private act. The act of encryption, in fact, removes information from the public realm. Even laws against cryptography reach only so far as a nation's border and the arm of its violence. Cryptography will ineluctably spread over the whole globe, and with it the anonymous transactions systems that it makes possible.

For privacy to be widespread it must be part of a social contract. People must come and together deploy these systems for the common good. Privacy only extends so far as the cooperation of one's fellows in society. We the Cypherpunks seek your questions and your concerns and hope we may engage you so that we do not deceive ourselves. We will not, however, be moved out of our course because some may disagree with our goals.

The Cypherpunks are actively engaged in making the networks safer for privacy. Let us proceed together apace.

Onward.

Eric Hughes, 9 March 1993

APPENDIX III:
COMPUTER LANGUAGES BASED ON NATURAL LANGUAGE

Bringing natural language into programming is a notion that existed almost from the beginning. But all prior attempts at human-readability, from FLOW-MATIC to Applescript, focused on a more technical level as domain of the conversation. Lexon focuses on a higher level, the business logic, and strives to leave all structural artifacts behind.

But note the longevity of most languages in this list.

Also note that **Structured English** and **Pseudo-Code** are more of an idea than clear rule sets and are not used to write actual programs. That is why they are not listed below.

FLOW-MATIC

Grace Hopper, Remington Rand, 1955 (discontinued)

https://archive.computerhistory.org/resources/text/Remington_Rand/Univac.Flowmatic.1957.102646140.pdf

```
(0)   INPUT INVENTORY FILE-A PRICE FILE-B ;
      OUTPUT PRICED-INV FILE-C UNPRICED-INV FILE-D ;
      HSP D .
(1)   COMPARE PRODUCT-NO (A) WITH PRODUCT-NO (B) ;
      IF GREATER GO TO OPERATION 10 ;
      IF EQUAL GO TO OPERATION 5 ;
      OTHERWISE GO TO OPERATION 2 .
(2)   TRANSFER A TO D .
(3)   WRITE-ITEM D .
(4)   JUMP TO OPERATION 8 .
(5)   TRANSFER A TO C .
(6)   MOVE UNIT-PRICE (B) TO UNIT-PRICE (C) .
(7)   WRITE-ITEM C .
(8)   READ-ITEM A ;
      IF END OF DATA GO TO OPERATION 14 .
(9)   JUMP TO OPERATION 1 .
(10)  READ-ITEM B ;
      IF END OF DATA GO TO OPERATION 12 .
(11)  JUMP TO OPERATION 1 .
(12)  SET OPERATION 9 TO GO TO OPERATION 2 .
(13)  JUMP TO OPERATION 2 .
(14)  TEST PRODUCT-NO (B) AGAINST ; IF EQUAL GO TO
      OPERATION 16 ; OTHERWISE GO TO OPERATION 15 .
(15)  REWIND B .
(16)  CLOSE-OUT FILES C ; D .
(17)  STOP . (END)
```

Fig 32 – FLOW-MATIC program code example

FLOW-MATIC was the first program language to use English words. It is the human-readable exponent of the 2nd generation of computer languages, which were usually content with looking like a jumble of three-letter abbreviations.

Grace Hopper described how they had to convince people of the advantage of human-readability[120] and how they chose the imperative form for verbs to be able to have a German version of FLOW-MATIC. It's not quite clear if this was a joke, the seemed to really want to go multi-lingual.

This language is where COBOL inherited its English-leaning roots from. The first COBOL compiler was written in FLOW-MATIC. COBOL, being of the next generation of program languages – the 3rd – soon replaced it.

Note the beauty of line 12. FLOW-MATIC is so close to machine code that it unabashedly modifies itself. This was de rigueur, as memory in the 50s was incredibly scarce and programs could be made shorter by modifying themselves in place.

The advantage that FLOW-MATIC achieved over what existed before was immense, as in the 50s programmers still operated with machine codes. Hopper described her own wrestling with octal numbers as a strong motivation to find a better way. Her arguments for 'B-0,' as she preferred to call FLOW-MATIC, were exactly the same that we are making for Lexon. But as the source example above betrays, the subject matter of FLOW-MATIC were still *cpu registers*, *files*, *atomic operations* and the *program pointer*. Hopper reasoned that FLOW-MATIC was not actually a *language*:

> *"The fact that we could substitute those French and English words means that it was never anything but a code. It was not a true language."*

> Grace Hopper[121]

---

[120] *"We finally convinced the Marketing Department that this could work. [..] to try and sell to the general public the idea of writing data processing programs in English statements. It was a long, torturous, and difficult job to get that concept accepted, because it was of course obvious that computers couldn't understand plain English, which made life very, very difficult."* – G. Hopper, https://dl.acm.org/citation.cfm?id=1198341

[121] G. Hopper, ibid.

COBOL

CODASYL, 1959

```
IDENTIFICATION DIVISION.
PROGRAM-ID. CONDITIONALS.

DATA DIVISION.
  WORKING-STORAGE SECTION.
  01 NUM1 PIC 9(9).

PROCEDURE DIVISION.
  MOVE 25 TO NUM1.

  EVALUATE TRUE
     WHEN NUM1 < 2
        DISPLAY 'NUM1 LESS THAN 2'
     WHEN NUM1 < 19
        DISPLAY 'NUM1 LESS THAN 19'
     WHEN NUM1 < 1000
        DISPLAY 'NUM1 LESS THAN 1000'
  END-EVALUATE.
  STOP RUN.
```

COBOL is one of the very first 3rd generation languages, probably the third, created in the late 50s and unbelievably, still around.

It was designed by committee with no computer scientists invited. They were left out because some people felt the ivory tower guys were intentionally dragging their feet on coming up with a language that would help standardize business programming. This didn't go down will in the academic community and COBOL was dissed hard from the very first moment.[122]

Yet by the 70s COBOL was the most widely used programming language in the world. Together with FORTRAN it is also the eldest language still in use: crazy 60 years now.

---

[122] COBOL was not even defined using the new and fashionable BNF.

Its English-like syntax was intended to make it self-documenting and easy to learn. Its optics have many detractors but there are also vocal defenders of COBOL who claim that it is still around because the closeness to English make it well maintainable. The criticism is that this also makes it very verbose.

COBOL has 300 reserved words and has a pronounced document structure of *divisions*, *sections*, *paragraphs* and *sentences*. Despite the similarity, the terms are not used in the same way as with Lexon.

COBOL was heavily influenced by its direct predecessor FLOW-MATIC and being a child of the 50s its optics are clearly that of a more or less cryptic-looking *program flow description*, not anywhere near to spoken English. Despite being standardized, COBOL has 300 dialects. It is still running on mainframe computers of big corporations today and seems to be very hard to replace – not that there would not be better ways to do things by now but it would ostensibly be very costly to switch. A major maintenance problem today is that COBOL programmers have started to die out. Literally.

The badmouthing of COBOL never stopped. Just say 'COBOL' and programmers trip over each other laughing. Then ask if they know even one line of COBOL. Pragmatic initiatives can be perceived as very offensive.

SQL

Chamberlin and Boyce, IBM, 1974

http://citeseerx.ist.psu.edu/viewdoc/download?doi=10.1.1.129.6517&rep=rep1&type=pdf

```
SELECT  isbn,
        title,
        price,
        price * 0.06 AS sales_tax
FROM    Book
WHERE   price < (SELECT AVG(price) FROM Book)
ORDER   BY title;
```

Fig 33 – SQL program code example

SQL is based on relational algebra and was made to describe datasets to be retrieved from a Relational Database like Oracle, DB2, or mySQL. SQL has a voluminous standard, but there are around 20 relevant dialects in the industry.

SQL is exclusively specialized for managing and accessing databases and since decades, the global top dog for it. Because of this, SQL is embedded in many other languages in more or less direct ways: even systems otherwise written in a 3rd generation language will usually query data from a Relational Database by using SQL commands that are embedded in the code in more or less elegant fashion. Usually horribly unelegant actually. But that shows how SQL is regarded as indispensable for the task of accessing a database.

SQL as a language is subdivided into several elements, including *clauses*, *expressions*, *predicates*, *queries* and *statements*. It can be described as super set of a number of specialized sub languages that deal in data definition, querying, controlling and manipulation, respectively. It is mostly a declarative language (4th generation language) as it describes *what* is wanted while leaving open *how* it should be found. It incorporates the typical 3rd generation elements of procedural programming though.

As can be seen in the example above, it is in fact possible to intuit the meaning of simple SQL code. This deteriorates quickly with more complex queries though, which need a *very* mathematical mind to comprehend.

In practice, middle management is articulating queries in SQL that are then checked and optimized by programmers to make sure that the queries are written in a performance-optimized way that will create as little load on the database system as possible.

Further underlining how the language SQL has become synonymous with the entire concept of Relational Databases, a wave of non-relational databases that emerged from 2009 was called "NoSQL" databases. In reality they were simpler data stores mostly tailored to the needs of web pages, shedding overhead of Relational Databases to gain performance and robustness. Some even kept SQL as their language. But because a database without SQL had become unthinkable by the earliest 21st century, "NoSQL" was the best way to express the advent of a different technological approach.

However, the resounding success of this kind-of somewhat-human-readable language reminds of the longevity of COBOL. They are both examples of how natural language-inspired computer languages can be wildly successful.

NATURAL

Peter Pagé, Software AG, 1975

https://www.softwareag.com/corporate/products/adabas_natural

```
DEFINE DATA
    LOCAL
    1 PERSONAL VIEW OF EMPLOYEES
    2 NAME
    2 CITY
END-DEFINE ;

FIND ALL RECORDS
    IN FILE PERSONAL
WITH NAME = 'SCHMIDT' ;
    DISPLAY NAME CITY ;
END-FIND ;
END
```

The programming language NATURAL was created for the ADABAS database system that is based on NF^2 [123] a holdout competitor to SQL databases. While its makers promise support through 2050, ADABAS is now not considered mainstream any more. But the noteworthy aspect here is in how much NATURAL *resembles* its bigger brother SQL with regard to borrowing from natural language.

ADABAS was developed to address the short comings of Relational Databases and SQL. Accordingly, NATURAL can do stuff SQL cannot and vice versa. But NATURAL is generally much broader in scope, e.g. including output formatting, and was originally designed to compete with COBOL on mainframes, i.e. the mainstream 3rd generation language at the time.[124] The term "4GL" (4th generation language) was actually created for ADABAS' marketing, as programs in NATURAL can be said to be describing a desired *outcome* rather than a *way* to solve it (3rd).

---

[123] Non-First Normal Form, also called Inverted List: Adabas stores some data non-normalized, as arrays – https://en.wikipedia.org/wiki/ADABAS

[124] http://tech.forums.softwareag.com/techjforum/posts/list/24345.page

As usual for a 4GL, NATURAL's focus is on database fields, queries and details of organizing data output. Today it supports all relevant operating systems and databases, ADA-BAS itself offers a SQL Gateway that provides access for tools like Crystal Reports and NATURAL is now seen more as a competitor of Java.

Like SQL, in simple examples, NATURAL reads very well.

HyperTalk

Dan Winkler, Apple, 1987 (discontinued)

http://hypercard.org/HyperTalk%20Reference%202.4.pdf

```
on mouseDown
    answer file "Please select a text file to open."
    if it is empty then exit mouseDown
    put it into filePath
    if there is a file filePath then
        open file filePath
        read from file filePath until return
        put it into cd fld "some field"
        close file filePath
        set the textStyle of character 1 to 10 of
                card field "some field" to bold
    end if
end mouseDown
```

HyperTalk was created for a forerunner of the web, the (offline) HyperCard software development system of early Apple computers.

It had an English-leaning vocabulary combined with a grammar modelled in the image of the procedural programming paragon Pascal.[125] Notably, it makes use of the pronoun "it" in a natural way, modelling one of the most demanding aspects of human language.[126]

HyperTalk was the first of the xTalk family of languages and had many successful heirs, among them LiveCode's Transcript, Flash's Actionscript, Applescript and Lingo.

---

[125] Pascal is a very clean 1970 language that was proposed to improve programming practices. It was used a lot in universities to teach programming and is a classic example of a 3rd generation language.

[126] Lexon has elements like this, in an even trickier way. They can be implemented because of the low level of Lexon's foundation. Meng Wong of the Legalese project remarked on that with 'envy' when first inspecting Lexon.

Applescript

Apple, 1993

```
tell application "Finder"
    set passAns to "app123"
    set userAns to "John"
    if the text returned of (display dialog
"Username" default answer "") is userAns then
         display dialog "Correct" buttons
    {"Continue"} default button 1
         if the text returned of
    (display dialog "Username : John" &
    return & "Password" default answer
    "" buttons {"Continue"} default
    button 1 with hidden answer) is
    passAns then
              display dialog "Access granted"
       buttons {"OK"} default button 1
          else
            display dialog "Incorrect password"
    buttons {"OK"} default button 1
          end if
     else
     display dialog "Incorrect username"
   buttons {"OK"} default button 1
     end if
end tell
```

Applescript is made to automate interaction between applications on the Mac. It uses the fact that Mac applications publish "dictionaries" of addressable objects and operations.

Applescript freely mixes procedural, object oriented and natural language. It has a quite 'natural' grammar that has the basic structure of an unnamed subject 'telling' applications what to do. But the complexity of parametrizing what that is, soon drowns out the initial similarity to spoken English.

Inform7

Graham Nelson, 2006

http://inform7.com

```
"Hello Deductible" by "I.F. Author"

The story headline is "An Interactive Example".

The Living Room is a room.
"A comfortably furnished living room."

The Kitchen is north of the Living Room.

The Front Door is south of the Living Room.
The Front Door is a door.
The Front Door is closed and locked.

The insurance salesman is a man in the Living
Room.
The description is "An insurance salesman in a
tacky polyester suit.
He seems eager to speak to you."
Understand "man" as the insurance salesman.

A briefcase is carried by the insurance
salesman.
The description is "A slightly worn, black
briefcase."
Understand "case" as the briefcase.

The insurance paperwork is in the briefcase.
The description is "Page after page of small
legalese."
Understand "papers" or "documents" or "forms"
as the paperwork.
```

Inform7 is a programming language to create text adventure games.

Its predecessor became a popular language to write interactive fiction in the late 90s. Based on that experience, its author created a complete rework of the language, that now nicely resembles natural language as can be seen above.

Inform7 is a niche language with a very special purpose, certainly a member of the 4th generation of computer languages, as there are no pointers in the code as to *how* the specification should be realized. Its output feeds into virtual machines for text adventures, which 'understand' e.g. the meaning of a 'closed door,' and how a player can interact with it. It's funny that this example includes a contract but there is no connection.

Inform7 is under active development and was set to be open-sourced in 2019.

Esoteric Languages

The term 'Esoteric programming languages' describes experiments and art projects.

Osmosian

Osmosian Order, 2006 (discontinued)

http://www.osmosian.com

```
The background is a picture.

A button has a box and a name.

To clear the status:
      Clear the status' string.
      Show everything.

To create the background:
Draw the screen's box with the white color.
Loop.
Pick a spot anywhere in the screen's box.
      Pick a color between the lightest gray
color and the white color.
      Dab the color on the spot.
If a counter is past 80000, break.
...


To run:
   Start up.
   Initialize our stuff.
   Handle any events.
   Finalize our stuff.
   Shut down.

To show everything:
   Hide the cursor.
   Draw the background.
   Draw the status.
   Draw the print button.
   Draw the quit button.
   Draw the text.
   Draw the current work.
   Refresh the screen.

To show a string in the status:
   Put the string into the status' string.
```

```
Show everything.

The status has a box and a string.

The text has a box and a string.

A work is a thing with a URL and a painting.

The works are some works.
```

Osmosian succeeds in having a zero-learning curve for readers, even though this example clearly stays within the realm of 3rd generation languages, due to its main concern being the low-level minutiae of screen output.

Osmosian has a clear philosophy and method that might be at the heart of its ongoing fascination:

> *"my power is rooted in my simplicity. I parse sentences pretty much the same way you do. I look for marker words — articles, verbs, conjunctions, prepositions — then work my way around them. No involved grammars, no ridiculously complicated parse trees, no obscure keywords. […]*
>
> *(1) I really only understand five kinds of sentences:*
>
> > *(a) type definitions, which always start with A, AN, or SOME;*
> >
> > *(b) global variable definitions, which always start with THE;*
> >
> > *(c) routine headers, which always start with TO;*
> >
> > *(d) conditional statements, which always start with IF; and*
> >
> > *(e) imperative statements, which start with anything else.*
>
> *(2) I treat as a name anything after A, AN, ANOTHER, SOME, or THE, up to:*
>
> > *(a) any simple verb, like IS, ARE, CAN, or DO, or*
> >
> > *(b) any conjunction, like AND or OR, or*

> (c) any preposition, like OVER, UNDER, AROUND, or THRU, or
>
> (d) any literal, like 123 or "Hello, World!", or
>
> (e) any punctuation mark.
>
> (3) I consider almost all other words to be just words, except for:
>
> (a) infix operators: PLUS, MINUS, TIMES, DIVIDED BY and THEN;
>
> (b) special definition words: CALLED and EQUAL; and
>
> (c) reserved imperatives: LOOP, BREAK, EXIT, REPEAT, and SAY."[127]

Github has a fork of OSMOSIAN that has commits from 2014 and 2017 but

> "is not endorsed by the Order."

Oh, good stuff, and so very mysterious. Lexon is less wild and genial, much more regular and meticulous. Its grammar leaves less space "for just words." OSMOSIAN is much closer to what Noam Chomsky suggests today about how natural languages, and our thought process, work. He has long left the Context-free Grammars behind that compiler compilers have been based on.

---

[127] http://www.osmosian.com/instructions.pdf

Metafor

Liu and Lieberman, MIT, 2005 (discontinued)

```
When a customer orders a drink, the bartender
tries to make it. When the bartender is asked
to make a drink, he makes it and gives it to
the customer only if the drink is in the menu's
drinks; otherwise, the bartender says "sorry i
don't know how to make that drink" to the
customer.128
```

Metafor was an experiment of using descriptions in natural language as starting point for the creation of programs.

> *"Every program tells a story. Programming, then, is the art of constructing a story about the objects in the program and what they do in various situations."*

Metafor whitepaper[129]

Metafor was not a language but an *intelligent user interface* with a knowledge base behind. A subset of English was designated as 'visualization tool' for the programmer. It accepted very free-floating English prose. Nouns were to be interpreted as program objects, verbs as functions, and adjectives as properties. The experiment was inspired by the observation how text-based adventures achieve usable interaction even with very simple template-based parsers, search engines and chatbots. The hope was that Metafor might help novice and intermediate programmers, in a 'scaffolding' step before the actual writing of the code.

---

[128] http://alumni.media.mit.edu/~hugo/publications/papers/IUI2005-metafor.pdf
[129] Ibid.

Legicode

Jacob Peddicord, 2006 (discontinued)

https://web.archive.org/web/20070109022136/http://legi-code.com/home/the-syntax

```
if the variable 'counter' is greater
than 5 then
show a message titled 'Greater than 5'
with the text 'It is greater than 5!'
if not then
end the program
end if
```

Legicode was a hobby project, intended as a beginners programming language. The idea was to lead towards 'real' programming by gradually switching over from the verbose starting point to a shorthand version of the same commands. So that a proficient writer of Legicode would eventually be writing in a style as brief as BASIC or Python.

The name was a play on *legible*, not on the law. It seems no indentation was envisaged.

Legicode's basic style is solid 3rd generation. The reading flow was perfect it seems – except for the marker to close the block: end if.

> *"This language will not have much usefulness
> in actual programming, but more simply as a way for
> newbie programmers to get started."*
>
> Jacob Peddicord

Shakespeare Programming Language

Jon Åslund, Karl Hasselström   (discontinued)

http://shakespearelang.sourceforge.net/report/shakespeare/

```
The Infamous Hello World Program.

Romeo, a young man with a remarkable patience.
Juliet, a likewise young woman of remarkable
grace.
Ophelia, a remarkable woman much in dispute
with Hamlet.
Hamlet, the flatterer of Andersen Insulting
A/S.

Act I: Hamlet's insults and flattery.

Scene I: The insulting of Romeo.

[Enter Hamlet and Romeo]

Hamlet:
 You lying stupid fatherless big smelly half-
witted coward!
 You are as stupid as the difference between a
handsome rich brave
 hero and thyself! Speak your mind!

 You are as brave as the sum of your fat little
stuffed misused dusty
 old rotten codpiece and a beautiful fair warm
peaceful sunny summer's
 day. You are as healthy as the difference
between the sum of the
 sweetest reddest rose and my father and
yourself! Speak your mind!

 You are as cowardly as the sum of yourself and
the difference
 between a big mighty proud kingdom and a
horse. Speak your mind.

 Speak your mind!

[Exit Romeo]


Scene II: The praising of Juliet.

[Enter Juliet]

Hamlet:
 Thou art as sweet as the sum of the sum of
Romeo and his horse and his
```

black cat! Speak thy mind!

[Exit Juliet]

Scene III: The praising of Ophelia.

[Enter Ophelia]

Hamlet:
 Thou art as lovely as the product of a large
rural town and my amazing
 bottomless embroidered purse. Speak thy mind!

 Thou art as loving as the product of the
bluest clearest sweetest sky
 and the sum of a squirrel and a white horse.
Thou art as beautiful as
 the difference between Juliet and thyself.
Speak thy mind!

[Exeunt Ophelia and Hamlet]

Act II: Behind Hamlet's back.

Scene I: Romeo and Juliet's conversation.

[Enter Romeo and Juliet]

Romeo:
 Speak your mind. You are as worried as the sum
of yourself and the
 difference between my small smooth hamster and
my nose. Speak your
 mind!

Juliet:
 Speak YOUR mind! You are as bad as Hamlet! You
are as small as the
 difference between the square of the
difference between my little pony
 and your big hairy hound and the cube of your
sorry little
 codpiece. Speak your mind!

[Exit Romeo]

Scene II: Juliet and Ophelia's conversation.

[Enter Ophelia]

Juliet:
 Thou art as good as the quotient between Romeo
and the sum of a small
 furry animal and a leech. Speak your mind!

Ophelia:
 Thou art as disgusting as the quotient between
Romeo and twice the

```
   difference between a mistletoe and an oozing
   infected blister! Speak
   your mind!

[Exeunt]
```

The Shakespeare Programming Language, like the Chef programming language, is designed to make programs *appear* to be something other than programs; in this case, Shakespearean plays (in the case of Chef, cooking receipts).

A *character list* in the beginning of the program declares a number of *stacks*, naturally with names like "Romeo" and "Juliet". These characters then enter into dialogue with each other in which they manipulate each other's topmost values, push and pop each other, and do I/O. The characters can also ask each other questions which behave as conditional statements. On the whole, the programming model is very similar to assembly language (a 70-year old 2nd generation language) but much more verbose.

It's really just fooling around.

NaturalJS

Elchanan Shor, 2018 (discontinued)

https://github.com/elshor/naturaljs/

```
DEFINE move to next token CONTEXT context AS
        context.currentToken =
    text.substr(context.currentPosition).match(/s*[
    \S]+); if(context.currentToken !== null){
            move the current position
        by (length of (context.currentToken));
    }
END

let context = {
        text : "hello world",
        currentPosition : 0,
        currentToken : null
};
move to next token;
show (context.currentToken);
move to next token;
show (context.currentToken);
```

Naturaljs was a proposal for a human-readable program language based on JavaScript. It would mix the definition of new keywords with JavaScript code snippets that defined them. Give it a star on Github to help it get started.

> "Naturaljs is a natural language programming extension to Javascript. Our goal is to provide a programming language as close as possible to natural language. We will do that by gradually adding natural language features to Javascript code and providing a parser that will identify the natural language islands in Javascript code and transpile them into Javascript.
>
> Elchanan Shor

APPENDIX IV:
CONSTRUCTED HUMAN LANGUAGES

A day after receiving a Lexon live demo, Gavin Wood – a driving force behind Ethereum, initiator of Solidity and founder and inventor of Polkadot – proposed to create a smart contract language based on the artificial human language *Loglan*.

That's missing the point of Lexon, which allows for readability without any preparation. Learning Loglan to be able to read smart contracts would be more involved than learning Solidity. The intuitive similarity lies in how Loglan has a regular grammar, unlike any natural language but very much like Lexon. And how Loglan should be able to express anything under the sun, as opposed to the pure programming language Solidity.

But a fundamental misunderstanding might arise regarding *in what sense* Lexon and constructed human languages, respectively, are regular. Lexon's grammar and restrictions are *very* much informed by programming paradigms, things like variable scope, control flow, matching, and object orientation. Constructed human languages, however, are often 'merely' focused on creating simpler, regular grammars that suit the purposes of a human speech, or thought. They do not bring the 'mapping' of concepts between language and programming that Lexon, as transparently as possible, proposes.

It may make sense to contrast Lexon with previous attempts at creating new human languages, to get a better grasp of Lexon's place in this wider context and what is new about it. David Bovil reasons that Lexon is an exponent of the new class of *performative languages*: communication that does not merely inform or suggest but directly causes things to happen. As such it should be seen not only in the context of programming languages.

Constructed natural languages were the forerunners of programming languages that try to achieve semblance of human speech. Hundreds of languages have been invented over time. The motivation has often been given as a deeply political one, but it is fair to assume that a strong linguistic passion drove all projects and communities. A common claim used to be the role Auxiliary Languages might have to promote world peace (Volapük, Esperanto, Basic English), by making people able to talk with each other. Another is the exploration of the relationship between language and thought (Newspeak and Loglan). George Orwell in particular was outspoken about how eliminating ambiguity would be a step down the road to tyranny. Through a role in business, as language for contracts, Lexon might influence natural language at some point. Orwell's warning deserves attention.

Another point of interest is how communities developing around language projects struggled with questions of consensus about contributions and copyright. Volapük and Loglan suffered heavily from it. Of the following list, only Esperanto really is alive.

Volapük

Martin Schleyer, 1879

http://volapük.com

> **O Fat obas, kel binol in süls,**
> **paisaludomöz nem ola!**
> **Kömomöd monargän ola!**
> **Jenomöz vil olik, äs in sül, i su tal![130]**

During a time when English had not achieved its prevalence, Volapük was the first successful artificial language designed to facilitate communication as a second language. It was not the first time the idea for a universal language was floated and not the first that was constructed. But it kicked off a wave.

Despite what the umlaut in its name suggests, Volapük's vocabulary was mostly derived from English, with some French and German stems mixed in. Schleyer aspired for the word origins to be brief and rather *not* recognizable so as to not alienate speakers of other nations. Volapük, for example, comes from 'world speak.' But the use of umlauts exposed it to the ridicule of English speakers.[131]

Schleyer claimed that God had instructed him to create an international language, which suggests some messianic drive to create and 'evangelize' the vision. Hundreds of Volapükist clubs existed around the globe in the 1880s and one million fans of the language were claimed at that time. But schisms[132] over the direction of further development led to

---

[130] The Lord's Prayer in Schleyer's 1880 rendition – https://en.wikipedia.org/wiki/Volap%C3%BCk

[131] https://www.berfrois.com/2012/12/truth-beauty-volapyk-arika-okrent

[132] https://en.wikipedia.org/wiki/International_Volap%C3%BCk_Academy

Volapük's rapid decline already at the end of the century when most students switched to the easier Esperanto.

Volapük inspired numerous other artificial languages, some very similar, some with no connection, and almost all forgotten. Today, Volapük is estimated to have 20 speakers globally. It still has its own Wikipedia [133] and academy. [134] But Schleyer no doubt succeeded in starting a movement.

> "In August 1889 the third convention was held in Paris. About two hundred people from many countries attended. And, unlike in the first two conventions, people spoke only Volapük. For the first time in the history of mankind ... an international convention spoke an international language."
>
> André Cherpillod

---

[133] https://vo.wikipedia.org

[134] http://volapük.com

Esperanto

Ludwik L. Zamenhof, 1887

http://esperanto.org

> Patro nia, kiu estas en la ĉielo,
> sanktigata estu Via nomo.
> Venu Via regno.
> Fariĝu Via volo
> kiel en la ĉielo, tiel ankaŭ sur la tero.

Esperanto is the most successful constructed human language with an estimated 100,000 speakers globally, 1 million people in the know and even around 1,000 native speakers today who learnt it from childhood.

Esperanto's vocabulary and grammar are based mostly on Latin, but it incorporates stems from other languages when they were found to be more popular across different languages. As a result, it is exceedingly simple to learn for someone versed in one Southern and one Northern European language. Esperanto is completely regular in its word endings, e.g. -o signifying nouns, -as verbs in present tense, -u imperative, -a adjectives. These choices give it a Mediterranean sound.

Esperanto, in Esperanto, means 'one who hopes,' which expresses the pacifistic spirit it was born from. Zamenhof's hope was that it could help prevent ghettoization, racism and war. After Esperantists were initially indexed and imprisoned by the thousands under Stalin, Esperanto was later supported by the states of the Eastern Block as alternative to English. It remains an optional high school subject in Hungry and can be studied at the university in Poland. A chair exists at the university of Amsterdam and the World Esperanto Association sits in Rotterdam with an office in the UN building in New York.

To facilitate exchange across borders, Esperantists have offered each other free accommodation since long before couch surfing. Today, the initial purpose of the language has been largely abandoned, acknowledging that English has become the world's lingua franca, and Esperantist culture has become a thing in itself.

> *"Diversity of languages is the first, or at least the most influential, basis for the separation of the human family into groups of enemies."*
>
> L. L. Zamenhof

Basic English

Charles K. Odgen, 1930

http://www.basic-english.org

> **Our Heavenly Father,**
> **may your name be glorified.**
> **May your kingdom come;**
> **may your will be done**
> **on earth as it is in heaven.**

Basic English intended to pare down English to a viable core, learnable in a mere 60 hours, that would still sound 'normal' to a native English speaker. It was proposed as auxiliary world language a hundred years ago and was promoted as tool for world peace in the 1950s. It serves as inspiration and learning tool today.

Basic English is a proper 'controlled language,' like Lexon, reducing the richness of English to a small and regular subset. The size of vocabulary deemed sufficient was found to be a mere 850 words,[135] a list that is still used internationally for teaching English. The Simple English Wikipedia[136] is based on the concept of Basic English but uses it only as a guideline that is not strictly enforced. It turned out to be quite difficult for teachers of Basic English to learn which rules and words were included and which not. A similar situation exists with Lexon but it might pose less of a challenge because Lexon is *more* restricted.

> *"What the World needs most is about 1,000 more dead languages—and one more alive."*
>
> Charles K. Odgen

---

[135] https://en.wiktionary.org/wiki/Appendix:Basic_English_word_list
[136] https://simple.wikipedia.org

Newspeak

George Orwell, 1949

http://orwell.ru/library/novels/1984/english/en_app[137]

> **Eat, drink,**
> **and be merry, for**
> **tomorrow we die.**

Newspeak is actually a fantasy language and was never meant to be used, but in an unexpected way it provides a link between Basic English and Loglan.

George Orwell had promoted Basic English in the 1940s before getting vocal about the negative consequences of a dumbed down language for the intellectual and political discourse.[138] His famous dystopian novel *1984* closes with a description of Newspeak, the language of the socialist dictatorship featured in *1984*.

Newspeak in Orwell's mind was *not "Freedom is Slavery"* or using *"Enhanced Interrogation Techniques"* as euphemism for torture. In his novel, he described Newspeak as designed by the dictatorship of Big Brother to make critical thought *impossible* by establishing as every day and only language a much reduced, strictly regular, and *less* ambiguous language.

Orwell was particularly critical of the attempt to eliminate double meaning, which he argued was the path to shallow, non-sensical, manipulative hollowness.

Newspeak was both a critique of the Soviet jargon of the time that Orwell had just fallen out of love with and the

---

[137] Note that the link to the free online copy of Orwell's original description of Newspeak from 1949 goes to a Russian domain hosted in Texas.

[138] Politics and the English Language, G. Orwell 1946: https://www.orwell.ru/library/essays/politics/english/e_polit/

contemporary use of English that he felt was becoming similarly appalling. He mixed artistic playfulness and political satire into the definition of Newspeak so that the language itself is probably less useful than Klingon and no one ever tried becoming fluent in it.

Implicitly, Orwell firmly subscribed to the idea that language shapes thought. So much so that restricting language would allow to restrict thought. His point was to highlight what we stand to lose if we let language be dictated to us, by force, fashion or best intentions.

> *"Modern English, especially written English, is full of bad habits which spread by imitation and which can be avoided if one is willing to take the necessary trouble. If one gets rid of these habits one can think more clearly, and to think clearly is a necessary first step toward political regeneration"*
>
> George Orwell

Loglan

James C. Brown, 1955-88

http://loglan.org

> Hoi Memio Farfu, ji vi le skatyhaa gu,
> Eo ga nu sentydju ga letu namci.
> I eo letu nu bragai fa fadkaa.
> I eo lotu nu furmoi ga nu durzo vi la Ter,
> ciuvi le skatyhaa.[139]

Loglan was made to be different from human languages, so as to proof the hypothesis of Linguistic Relativity, which holds that a different language should lead to different thoughts; that language was in fact the 'fabric of thought' as Wilhelm von Humboldt had proposed in 1820.

This take on language was ridiculed from the 1960s when the idea of a genetically anchored innate faculty to speak became mainstream, from which Context-free Grammars and BNF resulted: the universal way to describe computer languages. But Loglan, short for 'logical language,' was made to find if people think more logically when thinking in a more logically constructing language.

In order to not bring presuppositions into the thought process, Loglan has no distinction between verbs, subjects and objects, no notion of tense, numerus or gender. In this regard it uncannily matches Newspeak. Loglan also tries to *overcome* ambiguity. Its vocabulary was derived from the eight at the time most-spoken languages of the world.

---

[139] The Lord's Prayer https://math.boisestate.edu/~holmes/loglan.org/(drafts%20-%20not%20part%20of%20loglan.org)/the-lords-prayer.html

In Loglan, the meaning-carrying words require 'arguments' in specific order. Through this, the order of words acquires paramount importance, not unlike the way of listing the arguments of a function call in classic programming languages.

Loglan is so regular that texts written in it can easily and reliably be decomposed by a machine. Like for Lexon, grammar descriptions[140] exist that help to parse Loglan texts unambiguously. But in the case of Loglan the definition of the language does not result in an AST (pg. 95). The test that a computer *can* parse it is nothing but an exercise for the sake of proving the consistency of Loglan's grammar. Achieving the regularity of being parseable is itself the mission. There is no next step.

In fact, to create a Lexon dialect of Loglan, it would have to *be restricted* ('controlled'), like English is for Lexon, to 'map' it to the logic of programming languages.

Loglan has been heavily criticized for being based on a severely lacking understanding of 'logic,' not implementing predicate logic correctly and being unintentionally biased towards English in its choice of argument positions and meaning of gerunds. Copyright claims by Brown lead to a schism of the community that was healed only after his death.

But Loglan's vision has allure and it inspired many references in fiction. Maybe unsurprisingly, it turned out difficult to learn. It has dedicated scholars but probably no more than a dozen speakers, and thinkers.

---

[140] Proposed PEG file for Loglan as of 2019:
https://math.boisestate.edu/~holmes/loglan.org/holmes_stuff/loglan.py
PEG is an alternative to BNF and Holmes discusses the difference in
https://math.boisestate.edu/~holmes/loglan.org/holmes_stuff/fall2015lo-glanreport.pdf

Attempto Controlled English (ACE)

Norbert E. Fuchs, 1995-2013

http://attempto.ifi.uzh.ch

> A customer enters a card and a code.
> If the code is valid then the ATM accepts the card.
> The code is valid.
> Does the ATM accept the card?

Attempto Controlled English (ACE) may be the closest to Lexon. It sparked excitement in academia and in true Cypherpunk spirit, the guys let code talk.[141]

Like Basic English and Lexon, ACE reads like normal English but is in fact based on a strict subset of rules.[142] Like Lexon, ACE allows to freely add words and define them in the process of using them. ACE sentences are assertions of the form:

subject + verb + complements + adjuncts

Reaching beyond the purpose of Basic English or Loglan, ACE is about the *processing* of what is written in ACE, i.e. about what happens after the parsing. The major goal of ACE is to allow to *logically evaluate* texts consisting of such sentences, interpreted as first-order logic. Accordingly, it has elaborate rules about how sentences are composed into a text, defining conjunction like 'and' and 'or' as would be expected, while parsing existential and universal quantors[143] out of the individual phrases.

---

[141] ACE Parser (using Prolog, no less): https://github.com/Attempto/APE, AceWiki engine: https://github.com/AceWiki/AceWiki

[142] http://attempto.ifi.uzh.ch/site/docs/ace_nutshell.html

[143] 'at least for one X it is true that ...' and 'it is true for all X that ...'

The rules are pretty strict, and, like with Lexon – or legal prose for that matter – the wooden tone of ACE texts betrays them.

ACE then allows for queries: on the surface of it, plain English questions that it can answer based on the statements that came before. "Yes" for the example above, as the ACE tooling can correctly connect the anaphoric reference "The code" to the *first* sentence (sic).

ACE also allows for commands, of the form:

subject + "," + predicate + "!"

But they play a limited role within the framework of ACE.

This is where Lexon, being based on higher-order logic, takes it further, from the description of the logic of a domain to the mix of process description and data that is typical for programs. ACE is made for knowledge presentation, which is one half of programming. And while the essence of ACE texts can be compiled to discourse representation structures (DRS) – a representation of *first*-order logic – Lexon code is eventually compiled to imperative execution instructions that describe both the data and the process through which the data should be manipulated: i.e. an entire program.

> *"Attempto ['I dare'] was the motto of Norbert E. Fuchs when he started the Attempto project at the University of Zurich in 1995, defying 'has been tried, can't be done' statements of some big shots in the field of computer linguistics that Norbert had asked for advice."[144]*

---

[144] http://attempto.ifi.uzh.ch

Fantasy Languages

There are languages that have been constructed with less pretense. Two popular proponents stand out.

Quenya

John R. R. Tolkien, 1910-1955

http://www.elvish.org/resources.html

> Ilu vanya, fanya, eari,
> i-mar, ar ilqa ímen. Írima ye Númenor.
> Nan úye sére indo-ninya símen, ullume;
> ten sí ye tyelma, yéva tyel ar i narqelion,
> íre ilqa yéva nótina, hostainiéva, yallume:
> ananta úva táre fárea, ufárea!
> Man táre antáva nin Ilúvatar, Ilúvatar
> enyáre tar i tyel, íre Anarinya qeluva? [145]

Quenya is an Elven language that John R. R. Tolkien developed for his genre-defining fantasy novel Lord of the Rings. Tolkien was an Oxford philologist well versed in many languages and kept iterating on his inventions all his life. He spun deep, invented etymologies and cross-pollination stories for his creations and also modelled geometrically regular rune systems for them. The entire saga of the Lord of Rings was said to be but a background invented by Tolkien to give his languages a home.

Quenya was not necessarily intended to be spoken by anyone. Its remarkable design goal, instead, was beauty. Like Lexon, Quenya was created somewhat backwards:

---

[145] From Firiel's Song as discussed at https://folk.uib.no/hnohf/firiel.htm

"It had begun with a leaf caught in the wind, and it became a tree; and the tree grew, sending out innumerable branches, and thrusting out the most fantastic roots."

The Elven language community does not claim a higher purpose and neo-Quenya that proposes solutions for major gaps in Tolkien's proposals is an accepted fact of life. Especially since most of Tolkien's linguistic work was not published during his lifetime and his son kept tight lids on it, allowing only select scholars access who kept publishing about it, releasing additional details for decades, as invitation to a cultish philology of the evolution of the fantasy of one man.

The additions to the language that were created for the Lord of the Rings movies was somewhat controversial but eventually the mission-freeness might keep the community sane in its quest for a timeless, beautiful language.

Klingon

Marc Okrand, 1984

https://www.kli.org

> larghtlhuH He' yIn
> nobtun lojmItvam
> tlj chIrgh
> wIquvmoH
> vaj tlhIHqanglah chaw'ta'
> tIlegh
> paghmey je tu' wewmey largh yIn[146]

Klingon is a major viral hit and the ultimate lesson in what makes an artificial language successful: nerdiness, improvisation, stereotyping, dictatorship, artful over-the-top malice and being impossible to pronounce.

Klingon is the purported language of the main antagonist alien race of mankind in the science fiction universe of Star Trek. It was reverse-engineered to justify the non-sensical utterances Scotty (yes that Scotty) invented for a Klingon character half a decade earlier. As a surprise success, Okrand's Klingon dictionary then sold 250,000 copies and Klingon is now advertised as, by some measure, the most successful artificial language. Google and Minecraft have settings for Klingon. While a Klingon Wikipedia version was closed down by Jimmy Wales under controversy,[147] the number of real-world projects that play around with Klingon – like theatre plays, TV subtitles, translation services – still keeps growing.

---

[146] From the Klingon poem *Blankness of Soul* by David E. Howerthon – http://www.angelfire.com/ak/bhagwandave/pklingon.html

[147] https://meta.wikimedia.org/wiki/History_of_the_Klingon_Wikipedia

Klingon was made to sound brutish and war-like to fit, at different times, the perception of English speakers of Japanese, Russian and German. The language was created in playful defiance of common denominators of natural languages: e.g. it has no clear 'ah' sound and the very rare sentence structure object-verb-subject. It still has a very limited vocabulary geared to battle-field communication. Okrand was able to retain the final say about its canon.

Despite its runaway success, and multiple works of world literature being translated to Klingon, it is believed to have at most three dozen speakers. It's just too hard.

APPENDIX V:
BUILDING FROM
SOURCE

This is for programmers who are interested in supporting the development effort of the Lexon compiler.

Find the source and more details at this URL:[148]

https://gitlab.com/lexon-foundation/lexon-rust

Using the source code from the above repository, you can build the Lexon compiler from scratch, to inspect it, amend it, and contribute. It can help you to make Lexon usable on other OS-ses than Linux and Mac. Because it is written in Rust, the Lexon compiler is very portable and it should be possible to make it run on just about any platform. It has a very small footprint.

The compiler can also run directly in a browser, on most any device, at native speed, i.e. with the feel of an installed application to it. The repository includes the wraps to translate the compiler to WebAssembly (WASM). But this is not needed to build, try and execute the compiler locally on your machine.

---

[148] For more links and resources see pg. 147.

This source code would also be the starting point for implementing new natural languages or new blockchain targets. Both is super fun and neither brutally time-consuming nor difficult to get to an experimental stage, if you know a bit of Rust.

The grammar for controlled English is found in the file **lexon/src/lexon.pest**. The output for Solidity (for Ethereum) is produced in **lexon/src/solidity.rs**. The output for Sophia (for Aeternity) is produced in **lexon/src/solidity.rs**.

Compiler: Building & Running

Prerequisites

- curl
- git
- gcc
- rust nightly

Building

```
git clone https://gitlab.com/lexon-foundation/lexon-rust.git
cd lexon-rust
cargo build
```

Running

```
cargo run example.lex
```

Usage

```
lexon <lexon source file>
lexon <target format> <lexon source file>
```

Example

```
lexon --sophia example.lex
```

Options

```
<target format>:

        --pre           pre-compiler output

        --guigen        JSON data to drive the con-
                        tract manager

        --solidity      program to deploy to the
                        Ethereum blockchain

        --sophia        program to deploy to the
                        Aeternity blockchain
```

WASM Build

The compiler can be built into any web page using the WASM build at **npmjs.com/package/lexon-wasm**.

```
npm install lexon-wasm
```

Source at: **https://gitlab.com/lexon-foundation/lexon-wasm**.

APPENDIX VI:
CODE & TREES

Below, three ASTs are presented, each followed by the respective source code that they were built[149] from. First for a Lexon escrow contract. Second, for the Solidity source that is generated as output when the Lexon compiler processes the first. Third, an independent approach at the same problem, programmed natively in Solidity without any Lexon involved (cf. pg. 139). The last example may serve as contrast to see how much less readably structured Solidity looks when it is not generated from Lexon.

The point throughout is to demonstrate how the ASTs express roughly the same functionality but **on different levels of abstraction.** And how the Solidity ASTs are concerned with detailed that makes them lose the 'meaning' that is visible in the higher-level Lexon AST.

---

[149] AST graphs in this book were not created in an automated process but manually.

Lexon Code: Walk-Through

Lexon AST

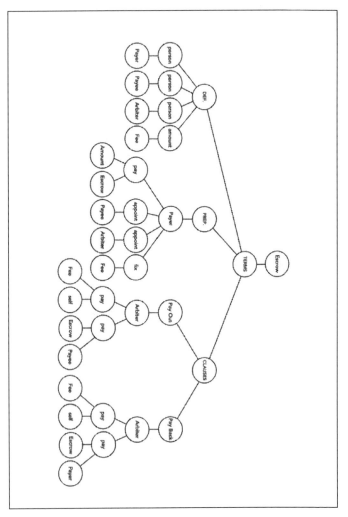

Fig 34 — Lexon AST for Escrow example (repeat of Fig 28)

This AST is best understood by comparing it to its Lexon code (pg. 370). The major parts (**DEF**[INITIONS], **RECIT**[ALS], **CLAUSES**) are positioned left to right in this AST, while in the source code they are appearing top to bottom, without explicit labels. A blank line is separating them.

The name of the program – or smart contract – is the label of the top-most node: **Escrow**.

The second AST level has only one node, the **TERMS**. The keyword **TERMS** is optional in some cases and therefore also missing in the source code for this example.

The next layer of the AST consists of the three parts of the **TERMS**: **DEFINITIONS**, **RECITALS** and **CLAUSES**. The **DEFINITIONS** start at **"Payer"**, the **PREPARATION** at **The Payer pays**, and the **CLAUSES** with the first **CLAUSE**. In the AST, the respective parts are simply everything under the node with respective label (**DEF.**, **RECIT.**, **CLAUSES**). The reason that labels of that name do not exist in the source is that they would be mostly redundant. The statements in the **DEFINITIONS** section looks a certain way, everything between them and the **CLAUSES** then are **RECITALS**. And each *individual* clause of course is marked by the keyword **CLAUSE**.

The source code is the best explanation for what the nodes and edges of the AST mean. For example, the left-most vertical in the AST, **DEF. –person–Payer** is the definition of the name **Payer** as a **person**. It is derived from the parsing of the line **"Payer" is a person**. After this, the meaning of the remaining nodes under **DEF.** is obvious.

In the AST, left of the center there is the vertical **RECIT.– Payer–pay–Amount**; with **Escrow** added under **pay**, too. This represents the source code **The Payer pays an Amount into escrow.** The remaining nodes under **RECIT.** follow the same logic. These lines are what is performed to set the contract up.

The AST verticals under **Pay Out** and **Pay Back** match **CLAUSE: Pay Out** and **CLAUSE: Pay Back** and are best explained by the source code below. **The Arbiter may,** signifies that *only* the **Arbiter** can invoke this clause. If anyone else tries, they will only get an error. The Arbiter is going to authenticate themselves with the private key that belongs to the blockchain address that is the basis for the identity of **Arbiter**. In Pay Out the **Arbiter** first **pays the Fee to themselves** that the **Payer** has set in the preparational phase of the contract performance. This **Fee** is paid from the escrow, i.e. deducted from the initial payment the **Payer made into escrow** during the Preparation. After the **Fee** is taken care of, the **remainder of the escrow** is sent to the **Payee**. **Pay Back** works the same with the one exception that the money goes back to the **Payer**.

LEX Paid Escrow.

"Payer" is a person.
"Payee" is a person.
"Arbiter" is a person.
"Fee" is an amount.

The Payer pays an Amount into escrow, appoints the Payee, appoints the Arbiter, and also fixes the Fee.

CLAUSE: Pay Out.
The Arbiter may pay from escrow the Fee to themselves,
and afterwards pay the remainder of the escrow to the Payee.

CLAUSE: Pay Back.
The Arbiter may pay from escrow the Fee to themselves,
and afterwards return the remainder of the escrow to the
Payer.

Fig 35 – Lexon Source Code for Escrow Example (repeat of Fig 1)

Generated Solidity: Walk Through

For completeness, this is the AST and source code of the Solidity code that is generated by the Lexon compiler from the Lexon Escrow example given above.

Generated Solidity: AST

The Solidity source that Lexon produces, of course loses the vocabulary and grammar of the Lexon code that it was created from. But it keeps the *document structure* and *names*. One can easily identify the four main branches again, now called **elements**, **construct**, **Pay Out** and **Pay Back**. But immediately below those, this AST shifts to a more granular, data-leaning concern and loses the clarity and all semblance to the Lexon AST.

As opposed to Lexon, there is no discernable subject-verb-object relationship. The code, and the tree, deal instead in permission details (**public**, **payable**, **private**) that are far from intuitive. It also takes care of requirements that arise from *variable scopes* (most of the **assigns**) and it is heavy on micro granular **calls** of functions and dereferencing of object elements (**lookup**). All these are purely programming-specific concerns that are not related to natural language. They dominate the shape of this AST.

To be clear, on the way from the Lexon code to the resulting smart contract running on the Ethereum mainnet, there are *two* compilation steps: from Lexon to Solidity, and from Solidity to *op codes* for the Ethereum virtual machine (EVM). Accordingly, an AST is created on two occasions: first the Lexon one shown above and then the Solidity one immediately below.

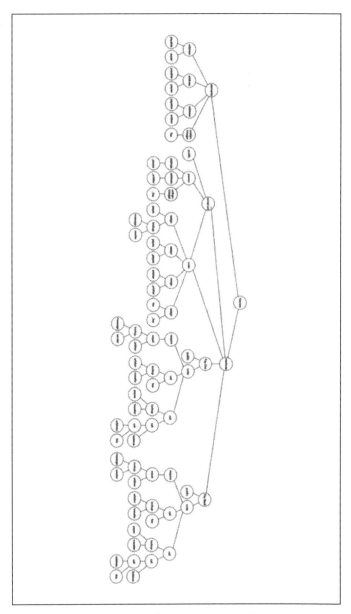

Fig 36 — Solidity AST for Escrow, Generated by Lexon

Generated Solidity: Source Code

```
pragma solidity ^0.5.0;

contract Escrow {
    address payable payer;
    address payable payee;
    address payable arbiter;
    uint fee;

    constructor(address payable _payee, address
payable _arbiter, uint _fee) public {
        payer=msg.sender;
        payee=_payee;
        arbiter=_arbiter;
        fee=_fee;
    }

    function PayOut() public {
        require(msg.sender == arbiter);
        arbiter.transfer(fee);
        payee.transfer(address(this).balance);
    }

    function PayBack() public {
        require(msg.sender == arbiter);
        arbiter.transfer(fee);
        payer.transfer(address(this).balance);
    }
}
```

Fig 37 — Solidity Source Code for Escrow, Generated by Lexon

It is relative straight forward to match Solidity AST nodes and
Solidity source code. And also, to understand their respective
meaning from the Lexon source code shown before.

Native Solidity: Walk Through

For comparison, the following is an abbreviated version of a third party example for an Solidity escrow contract.[150] It was chosen because its maker could not have any knowledge of Lexon and it illustrates well how different a 'hand-made' Solidity smart contract is *structured* that tackles pretty much the same task, i.e. implementing a simple escrow on the blockchain.

The graph below depicts the same tree as the one shown as Fig 29 on pg. 140, it is merely re-arranged for readability.

Expectably, as can be seen from the source code given below (Fig 39), this smart contract source has a different roster of functions: beyond the **constructor**, they are **deposit**, **accept**, **cancel** and **kill**. These names, of course, appear as main nodes in the AST below.

The function **deposit** is used to pay into the escrow. **accept** is a combined entry point to give consent to the pay out and to actually facilitate it, **cancel** is a similarly structured function to allow for the unanimous termination of the agreement, paying the money back. **kill** allows the controller of the escrow to terminate the agreement.

This code is yet heavier than the Lexon-generated Solidity (cf. above Fig 37, pg. 373) regarding the use of conditional branching (**if**), de-referentiation (**lookup**) and function **calls**.

This source does of course not share the document structure of the Lexon code example above. It has its own sequence and logic, and this highlights the lower level of abstraction that is applied when writing Solidity code.

---

[150] Pranav K. – https://medium.com/@pranav.89/smart-contracting-simplified-escrow-in-solidity-ethereum-b19761e8fe74

Native Solidity: AST

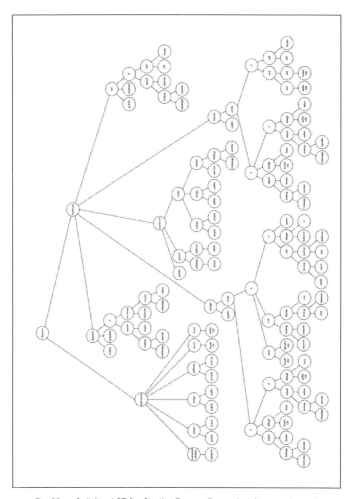

Fig 38 — Solidity AST for Similar Escrow Example (alternate layout)

Native Solidity: Source Code

```solidity
contract Escrow {

    uint balance;
    address public buyer;
    address public seller;
    address private escrow;
    bool buyerOk;
    bool sellerOk;

    constructor(address _buyer,
      address _seller) public {
        buyer = _buyer;
        seller = _seller;
        escrow = msg.sender;
    }

    function accept() public {
        if (msg.sender == buyer){
            buyerOk = true;
        } else if (msg.sender == seller){
            sellerOk = true;
        }
        if (buyerOk && sellerOk){
            // we are sending ourselves
            // (contract creator) a fee
            escrow.transfer(this.balance /100);
            if (seller.send(this.balance)) {
                balance = 0;
            } else {
                throw;
            }
        }
    }

    function deposit() public payable {
        if (msg.sender == buyer) {
            balance += msg.value;
        }
    }

    // if both buyer & seller would like
    // to cancel, money is returned
    // to buyer
    function cancel() public {
        if (msg.sender == buyer){
            buyerOk = false;
        } else if (msg.sender == seller){
            sellerOk = false;
        }

        if (!buyerOk && !sellerOk){
            selfdestruct(buyer);
        }
    }
```

```
function kill() public constant {
    if (msg.sender == escrow) {
        selfdestruct(buyer);
    }
}
}
```

Fig 39 – Solidity Source Code for Similar Escrow Example

INDEX

FIGURES

AUTHOR

Henning is the founder and CEO of the Lexon Foundation, he has been called many things and also a pioneer and thought leader in the blockchain space.

Henning was the first technical architect for IBM's blockchain, Hyperledger Fabric, wrote the first book on Ethereum, conducted blockchain research for the European Commission and architected the Diamond Blockchain for DeBeers as Director for Blockchain at the Boston Consulting Group.

Henning ran into the Ethereum people in Berlin in 2014 while working on his Bitcoin prediction market startup. He helped debugging Ethereum race conditions for IBM and worked as liaison between the Ethereum hackers and IBM developers.

Henning developed his first crypto application in 2001 and is a long-time contributor to open source. His long experience as a freelancer supplied him with useful knowledge about the real world. He worked in mobile payment, distributed databases, functional languages and computer language design: all areas which figure heavily in blockchain technology today.

Henning professionally used 18 different programming languages and created a language for the insurance industry that became a de facto standard. He is a second-generation hacker: his father happily programmed ALGOL 60 on a Z 23.

Henning gave keynotes and talks on five continents. Some people say they love his books, which is rad.

Reach him at **hd@lexon.tech**

#x2j

Writing a book is a journey,
one does not return the same person.

I always held back from reading the *Glass Bead Game*
to retain an open mind, the wonder and the curiosity
what it might be that Hesse unveils as the game that
can describe, in a language of colored marbles, any
work of art or science. That would allow to even
translate across the arts, a picture into a song:
obviously, a language of perfect abstraction.

One day I would read & find out.

But I ran into the spoiler, researching this book, that
the master's papers do not actually explain the game.

Hesse's novel was not, as I had thought, about a
fantastic exercise of insight and thought.

Not about his take on Leibniz' universal language.

It was about the danger of intellectual stagnation.
It was a call to action.

It expressed the warning that the world of thought was
grinding to a halt, rendered impotent by its infatua-
tion with superficial, self-indulgent games.

By being content with life in the ivory tower,
musing about the world instead of shaping it.

He started to write in 1930
and tried to publish it in 1943.

Access to Iustice is not a luxury problem.
It just looks that way from our walled gardens.

Printed in Germany
by Amazon Distribution
GmbH, Leipzig